LIGUORI CHRISTIAN INITIATION P[illegible]

FOR ADULTS

INQUIRY LEADER GUIDE

***Journey of Faith for Adults Inquiry Leader Guide* (826269)**

Imprimi Potest: Stephen T. Rehrauer, CSsR, Provincial, Denver Province, the Redemptorists

Imprimatur: "In accordance with CIC 827, permission to publish has been granted on May 31, 2016, by the Rev. Msgr. Mark S. Rivituso, Vicar General, Archdiocese of St. Louis. Permission to publish is an indication that nothing contrary to Church teaching is contained in this work. It does not imply any endorsement of the opinions expressed in the publication; nor is any liability assumed by this permission."

To order, visit Liguori.org or call 800-325-9521.

Contributing writers and editors of 2016 *Journey of Faith for Adults Inquiry Leader Guide:* Denise Bossert and Julia DiSalvo. Portions adapted from *Your Faith,* a Redemptorist Pastoral Publication, © 1993 Redemptorist Publications and © 2004 Liguori Publications; *On Baptism* translated by Rev. S. Thelwall, from Ante-Nicene Fathers, Vol. 3, edited by Alexander Roberts, James Donaldson, and A. Cleveland Coxe (Buffalo, NY: Christian Literature Publishing Co., 1885). Design: Lorena Mitre Jimenez. Images: Shutterstock.

Compliant with *The Roman Missal, Third Edition.*

Printed in the United States of America
20 19 18 17 16 / 5 4 3 2 1
Third Edition

Contents

Welcome to Journey of Faith!

Liguori Publications is dedicated to providing parishes with quality resources like *Journey of Faith*. Since 1993, *Journey of Faith* has established itself as a trusted and beloved program for catechists to guide participants through the RCIA process. As the Catholic Church takes on the challenges and graces of each generation, *Journey of Faith* has been carefully developed to help you meet the changing needs of adults, teens, and children who are inquiring about and seeking initiation into the Catholic Church—ever ancient, ever new.

The *Journey of Faith* program is cohesive, comprehensive, and flexible. *The Word Into Life* provides you with the *Lectionary* texts from Sunday Mass, and the forty-eight catechetical lessons and corresponding *Leader Guides* create a practical and attractive formation process for today's team leaders, catechists, and participants. All the materials are referenced to the *Catechism of the Catholic Church* and have been granted an *imprimatur* from the Archdiocese of St. Louis.

Unbaptized children over the age of seven are to be considered catechumens. Liguori offers any child or teen needing formation or sacraments *Journey of Faith for Children* and *Journey of Faith for Teens.* With the exception of the *Word Into Life* volumes, all *Journey of Faith* products are available in Spanish under the title *Jornada de fe.*

We hope you enjoy using *Journey of Faith* and find it enlightening and engaging for all. To see our entire collection of sacramental preparation titles, parish subscriptions, formation and spirituality books, and more, please visit Liguori.org to contact us for a copy of the latest catalog.

—The editors

An Overview of the RCIA

The Historical Development

The decision to become a member of the early Christian community bore serious ramifications. Becoming Christian meant a break with one's background and often required fracturing relationships with the non-Christian members of one's family. In many cases, this decision meant a willingness to suffer persecution or even death, as seen in the example of the martyrs Perpetua and Felicity. Perpetua, a noblewoman of Carthage and mother of an infant son, and Felicity, a pregnant slave woman, both refused to denounce Christianity and were subsequently martyred during the public games in the amphitheater around AD 200.

Just as the decision to become a Christian was not made lightly, the formation process wasn't quick or easy. Catechumens—those in the process of preparing for baptism—were invited into a step-by-step journey of three or more years with the community before achieving full membership. During this process, they were expected not only to begin to accept Christian beliefs but also to begin to live the Christian life. The community shared their faith with the catechumens and celebrated each step along with them.

One period of this preparation has remained throughout the centuries: the season of Lent. Originally this time was one of immediate preparation for baptism, which was celebrated at the Easter Vigil. During Lent, the entire Christian community, especially the catechumens, devoted themselves to prayer, fasting, and self-scrutiny. For those already baptized, it was a time to remember and renew their original commitment.

During the solemn Easter Vigil, the catechumens—now called the elect—received the sacraments of initiation (baptism, confirmation, and Eucharist) and were welcomed into the community. As a rule, this initiation was celebrated at the Easter Vigil only. Formation of the newly baptized did not end with the rites of Holy Saturday night, however, but continued with further instruction and daily living out of Christian values.

This process began to change in the fourth century, when periodic persecution of Christians was replaced by tolerance. Because of the favor many emperors showed toward it, Christianity became fashionable, and many people began entering the catechumenate for social and political reasons. As a result, the pattern and standards for formation gradually transitioned to the point where, by the fifth century, the rites of initiation were separated into the three sacraments we know and celebrate today. Infant baptism became the norm, and the catechumenate vanished.

The Church published the first *Roman Catechism* in 1566, following the Council of Trent. This book of teachings was presented in question-and-answer form and was used for instruction of the faithful. Such catechisms later became the foundation for what came to be called "convert classes." Using a teacher-student model, the priest would meet with interested parties and assist them in memorizing certain prayers and learning the material in the catechism. The duration of the process, the material to be covered, and the format were left to the priest or parish custom, with few outside directives given.

Successful completion of these classes meant either baptism or formal reception into the Catholic Church. This event was usually celebrated in a private ceremony, with only close family in attendance. Those received into the Church would be confirmed by the bishop at the cathedral or would receive the sacrament in their local parish whenever the bishop came to confirm the schoolchildren. Follow-up for the new Catholics, if any, might consist of being sent to a formal course in liturgy, Scripture, dogma, or morality.

Following World War II, a call for a change in the formation of new Catholics came from the Church in Africa. They began to use the ancient form of the catechumenate to provide stability in formation and a period of time for faith to mature. The Second Vatican Council in the 1960s called for a thorough revision of all the rites (Constitution on the Sacred Liturgy *[Sacrosanctum Concilium]*, 4), and a committee was formed that engaged in a formal study and revision of the methods leading to baptism or reception into the Catholic Church. This study resulted in the promulgation of the *Rite of Christian Initiation of Adults* (RCIA) in 1972.

Thus the catechumenate was restored: a process of formation, sanctified by various liturgical rites that mark progress in the journey of faith and culminate in full membership in the Catholic Christian community. An integral part of the revision is that the whole process and its rites are to be celebrated with and in the context of the local parish community and diocese.

The Scholastic or Ongoing Catechumenal Model

The catechumenate is considered a *process*, rather than a *program*, because it is a spiritual journey that varies according to time, place, and individual needs. It primarily focuses on:

- *Faith development* (rather than mastery of doctrine) and maturing in one's relationship with God.
- *Building and nourishing relationships*, not only among the participants and leaders but within the parish community and the universal Church.

Most U.S. parishes follow an academic schedule that begins in September and runs through May. However, this approach can make the process feel forced, rushed, or like a course of study that focuses on the *content* of the faith rather than the participant's experience of a *deepening conversion* and growing commitment. For this and other reasons (for example, risking that the *Catechism* becomes the main "course text" rather than the *Lectionary*), many pastoral ministers prefer an ongoing model for the process. *Journey of Faith* can be applied well to a number of models and provides a built-in flexibility that supports many formats.

Flexibility is one of the greatest assets of the RCIA. Within certain parameters, the pastor is given the freedom to accommodate the rites according to his judgment in order to fit the needs of the participants and parish. You, as catechists and team leaders, are encouraged to use your judgment in developing a process suited to the needs of both catechumens and candidates.

The Periods

This section provides detailed information on the periods of the RCIA. A basic orientation to the RCIA process is included in lessons Q1, "Welcome to the RCIA," and C1, "The RCIA Process and Rites." Together these lessons build a foundation for the participants as they begin their faith formation. The corresponding lesson plans support you, the leader, and offer program-specific notes.

Evangelization and Precatechumenate (Inquiry)

The first period is called *inquiry* or the *precatechumenate*. During this period, inquirers form relationships with one another and with their catechists. The sessions are informal and often center upon the life stories that have led each member there with questions such as:

- What is faith?
- Who is God, and why does God care about me?
- How does the Church understand the Bible and the sacraments?
- What are the roles of Mary and the pope?
- Why are there statues in Catholic churches?

Each inquirer will examine the Church and the ways in which its members worship together and live the Christian faith. First impressions of the parish and of all involved are very important. The period culminates in the inquirer's decision to enter the catechumenate, the period of formal preparation for entrance into full membership in the Catholic Church.

Catechumenate

The *rite of acceptance* marks the beginning of the catechumenate, a period of study and reflection on the faith. At this point, the inquirers become catechumens. Candidates (those already baptized but preparing for full membership in the Catholic Church) formally enter the RCIA process through the *rite of welcoming*. Both publicly state their intention to continue their formation, and the community supports them in their journey. Sponsors will act as companions and models of faith and lend their personal support.

The length of this period is determined by the needs of each participant and of the community. It can last anywhere from several months to a couple of years. During this time, the catechumens and candidates:

- learn Catholic beliefs
- are exposed to various forms of prayer
- join the community in worship, social events, and charitable activities
- participate in the apostolic life of the Church.

During the catechumenate, catechesis usually takes place during the Sunday liturgy. The participants are prayerfully dismissed after the Universal Prayer (Prayer of the Faithful); the catechists, and sometimes the sponsors, join them in reflecting upon the day's readings and connecting them to their faith and the life of the Church (see section *The Word Into Life*).

> *There should be celebrations of the word of God that accord with the liturgical season and that contribute to the instruction of the catechumens and the needs of the community... Celebrations of the word may also be held in connection with catechetical or instructional meetings of the catechumens, so that these will occur in a context of prayer.*
>
> *RCIA* chapter of *The Rites, Volume One (RCIA), 81, 84*

Purification and Enlightenment

When the catechumens and candidates are ready to make a formal request for the sacraments of initiation, and when the catechists and godparents are ready to recommend them to the bishop and to the parish community for full membership, the *rite of election* is celebrated. This celebration is generally held on the first Sunday of Lent. The rite of election marks the beginning of the *period of purification and enlightenment*, the time of immediate preparation for initiation or full reception at the Easter Vigil. (*Journey of Faith* refers to this period simply as enlightenment.)

The beginning of Lent signals a forty-day "retreat" in which the parish joins the elect in preparing for the mysteries celebrated at the Easter Vigil. The RCIA sessions are marked by increased emphasis on prayer and the interior life rather than on accumulation of knowledge. Many parishes allow time for a day of prayer especially designed for the elect and their supporters. On the third, fourth, and fifth Sundays of Lent, the scrutinies are celebrated during the liturgy. These rites are prayers of healing in which the elect, as well as the faithful, are reminded that everyone needs continued healing, conversion, and reconciliation.

Postbaptismal Catechesis (Mystagogy)

- The Easter Vigil does not mark the end of the RCIA process but the beginning of a commitment to a lifelong discovery and living out of the Catholic Christian tradition. The fifty days from Easter to Pentecost are called the period of *mystagogy*, a Greek word meaning "entering into the mysteries." In the early Church, this time was used to explain the mysteries of the sacraments. Today this period serves as a time for today's neophytes (newly converted) to:

- continue to gather, pray, and nourish their faith
- deepen their experiential understanding of God's word and the sacraments
- center more on the apostolic or social justice aspects of Catholic Christianity
- claim a new role of service in the community. (All Catholics are invited to active participation in parish life, which includes worship, stewardship, and fellowship.)

Sponsors and Godparents in the RCIA

> "A person to be baptized is to be given a sponsor who assists an adult in Christian initiation...A sponsor also helps the baptized person to lead a Christian life...."
>
> *Code of Canon Law* 872

Prior to the rite of acceptance, (RCIA) sponsors should be chosen for all catechumens. Sponsors represent the parish community and assist the larger Church in preparing the catechumen for baptism (here, initiation), testifying to his or her faith, and promising to assist him or her in living the Catholic faith.

Canon 874 lists the basic criteria for sponsors. These guidelines are the same for baptismal godparents and confirmation sponsors, though the roles are somewhat different:

1. The sponsor should be designated or invited by the catechumen or candidate.
   If he or she doesn't have someone in mind, the RCIA leader(s) or pastor will select an appropriate person from a voluntary pool of parishioners. This is similar to parents choosing godparents at the time of their child's baptism.
2. The sponsor must be at least sixteen years old—in other words, mature enough to understand and fulfill this important role.
3. The sponsor must be a confirmed Catholic "who leads a life of faith"—someone who has already committed to and experienced the Catholic faith journey.
4. No sponsor can be subject to a Church penalty such as excommunication.
5. The sponsor cannot be the participant's parent.

In the case of infant baptism, the parents already have a unique and important role to play. Some adult catechumen desire to have their spouse or a close friend or relative as a sponsor. This is generally discouraged, but RCIA leaders and pastors can help the catechumen decide whether the potential sponsor is sufficiently experienced and objective to fulfill this role.

RCIA leaders should develop a list of parishioners who are willing to become sponsors and maintain those connections as new inquirers arrive each year. It is important for sponsors with no prior relationship to the catechumen to realize that they are committing to an *ongoing* spiritual relationship. While their ecclesial role technically ends at the rite of election, sponsors often serve as, or stand in for, godparents, whose support lasts a lifetime.

Godparents are chosen before the rite of election (*RCIA* 123). Like sponsors, they will encourage, inspire, and even hold the elect accountable to remain faithful to Christ. Whenever possible, encourage the catechumens to use their RCIA sponsor as a baptismal godparent. Additional guidance for godparents can be found in the *Journey of Faith for Teens, Catechumenate Leader Guide.*

The Rites

Rite of Acceptance Into the Order of Catechumens

This rite marks the first transition in one's journey—the move from being an interested inquirer to an active catechumen. (For candidates seeking full communion in the Church, the *rite of welcoming* is used. *RCIA* 507 and the following details the combined rite.) The importance of this step is rightly recognized by the Church.

1. Symbolizing movement into the community, those asking to be received, along with their sponsors, begin by standing at the doors of the church (*RCIA* 48). The celebrant introduces them to the worshiping community, and asks, "What do you ask of the Church?" They state their desire for initiation, implying their intent to live, learn, and love with the community.
2. The sign of the cross is marked on each forehead, symbolizing the love and strength of Christ that accompanies each person (*RCIA* 54–55). This sign of faith may also be marked on their:
    a. ears (to hear the Lord's voice),
    b. eyes (to see God's glory),
    c. lips (to respond to God's word),
    d. heart (that Christ may dwell there),
    e. shoulders (to bear the gentle yoke of Christ),
    f. hands (that their work witnesses to Christ), and
    g. feet (to walk in Christ's way) (*RCIA* 56).
3. After the signing, catechumens and sponsors are formally invited to enter the church and to join in the celebration of the Liturgy of the Word (*RCIA* 60). Following the homily, the catechumens should be called forward and dismissed with a book of the Gospels or a cross (*RCIA* 64). They are specially included in the Mass' intercessory prayers before being formally dismissed from the assembly in order to pray and reflect upon the Scriptures (*RCIA* 65–67).

Other Rites in the Catechumenate

Other liturgical rites during this period, although optional, are significant to the continuing faith development of both participants and parishes:

- celebrations of the word of God (*RCIA* 81–89)
- minor exorcisms (*RCIA* 90–93)
- blessings (*RCIA* 95–96)
- anointing (*RCIA* 98–101)
- sending (*RCIA* 106–17)

Rite of Election

The importance of this rite is accented by the fact that it is often celebrated by the bishop (or bishop's representative) at the diocesan cathedral. The transition is marked further by a change of title and in the selection of the godparent(s) beforehand.

After the catechumens have been presented to the bishop and approved by the assembly (*RCIA* 130–31), their names are inscribed in the *Book of the Elect* (*RCIA* 132). Intercessory prayers and a special blessing for the elect follow this sacred moment.

The Scrutinies

1. The first scrutiny takes place on the third Sunday of Lent. Its focus is the story of the Samaritan woman at the well (John 4:5–42). After special intercessory prayers, the celebrant prays that the elect may be exorcised from the powers of sin (*RCIA* 150–156). During the week that follows, the presentation of the Creed should be formally made, preferably after a homily within Mass (*RCIA* 157–163).

2. The second scrutiny takes place on the fourth Sunday of Lent. It focuses on the story of the man born blind (John 9:1–41). Again, after the intercessions, the celebrant prays that the elect may be exorcised from the powers of sin (*RCIA* 164–170).

3. The fifth Sunday of Lent brings the Third Scrutiny. This Sunday focuses on the raising of Lazarus (John 11:1–45). Intercessory prayers from the worshiping community and prayers of exorcism from the celebrant again follow (*RCIA* 171–177). During the following week, the Presentation of the Lord's Prayer should be made, preferably after the reading of the Lord's Prayer from Matthew's Gospel. Following the homily, the celebrant calls on the community to pray silently for the elect. Before their dismissal, the celebrant bestows a special blessing upon the elect (*RCIA* 178–184).

Rites of Preparation

When it's possible to bring the elect together on Holy Saturday for reflection and prayer, these rites may be used in immediate preparation for the reception of the sacraments (*RCIA* 185 and following). If the *presentation of the Creed* or the *presentation of the Lord's Prayer* has not been celebrated already, they could be celebrated now. An *ephphetha rite* (a rite of opening the ears and mouth, symbolizing the hearing and proclaiming of the word) is a fitting preparation rite, as is the rite of *choosing a baptismal name*. Any or all of these rites serve to set the stage for the highlight of the RCIA experience: the sacraments of initiation.

Sacraments of Initiation

After months or years of sharing the faith, the RCIA journey culminates in this very special parish celebration. Holy Saturday is the night to celebrate, and the Church celebrates in style. In the early Church the Easter Vigil lasted until dawn; today's vigil lasts only a few hours (depending on the parish, generally between two and four). It is the most glorious celebration of the entire liturgical year.

1. This night begins in total darkness. The parish community may assemble outside for the blessing of the fire. Then, as the celebrant processes into the church, proclaiming the *Light of Christ*, each person lights a taper from the new Easter candle that has been blessed and ignited with the new fire. Soon the church is aglow with flame.

2. The Liturgy of the Word begins in candlelight. There are seven readings from the Old Testament provided, but it is not necessary to proclaim all seven. Psalms are interspersed between each reading.

3. Before the New Testament epistle is read, the *"Gloria"* rings out, the altar candles and electric lights are lit, and the Church bells are joyously rung. With this, the glorious *"Alleluia,"* the Gospel, and the homily, the stage is set for the sacraments of initiation.

4. The rite of baptism begins with the calling forth of those to be baptized. A litany of the saints follows, and the celebrant blesses the water by plunging the Easter candle into the baptismal pool. Baptism follows, and the newly baptized are clothed in white garments.

5. Once the baptisms are concluded, the candidates are called forward to profess their belief in the holy Catholic Church. They join the newly baptized, and the rite of confirmation is celebrated with the laying on of hands and anointing with chrism. Then the whole assembly renews their baptismal vows and the celebrant ritually sprinkles everyone with the newly blessed waters of baptism.

6. The Mass continues with the Universal Prayer and Liturgy of the Eucharist. When it's time to receive Communion, the new Catholics—along with their godparents, sponsors, catechists, and family members—lead the congregation in the eucharistic feast. This is the culmination of initiation: sharing at the table and being sent forth.

Traits of an Effective RCIA Team Member or Catechist

You don't have to be a theology professor or an experienced minister to be a successful catechist. Certain traits and techniques can make the process of faith formation easier and more enjoyable.

- ***Meet regularly throughout the process.*** Several weeks before the start of a new program or upon the arrival of a new inquirer, review the materials and determine where and when to hold the sessions. Good planning ensures that the process goes smoothly.
- ***Be flexible.*** Resist the temptation to create a precise schedule. Remain open to the workings of the Spirit in those who present themselves. Each session should include an opportunity for unfinished or previous business to be addressed. Often questions come up between sessions that were not apparent during your time together.
- ***Make each team member aware of the topics discussed***, materials covered, and questions raised in each session so there will be continuity among sessions and presenters. Contact the next session's presenters and brief them on any issues that surfaced or may need to be addressed.
- ***Link your presentations and discussions to their life experience.*** Catechists and team members are co-learners, catalysts, and partners—not directors. Openly sharing the stories of your own faith journey makes the participants more comfortable in accepting and sharing who and where they are.
- ***Be attentive and receptive.*** Communication, especially active listening, is one of your greatest tools in establishing trust. Look at the person and give him or her your undivided attention. Try to hear and to be open to what is said as well as any feelings underneath.
- ***Practice empathy and sensitivity.*** This requires a compassionate attitude and an awareness of your reactions and prejudices. Accept and affirm the uniqueness of each individual and genuinely desire to feel *with* him or her. The rest of the group will follow your example.
- ***Take advantage of opportunities for renewal and training.*** Faith is a relationship. While routines and habits are helpful, don't live by a script. Remain open to the opportunities and creative diversions of the Spirit. Above all, make time for your own spiritual growth. Take time daily for prayer. Practice the faith you share. Grow in Christ. Stay informed on new teachings and trends in the Church. Attend retreats and seminars and read books that develop your understanding and ministry skills. Be as present in the sacraments and active in the life of the parish as you hope your catechumens and candidates will be.
- ***Form a hospitality team.*** This team will provide snacks and beverages at each session and a well-planned and generously provided menu for the Easter Vigil retreat. This team does not need to stay for the sessions. In fact, they may wish to remain anonymous until the retreat, which becomes an opportunity for team members to reveal themselves and Christ's love in action.
- ***Establish an intercessory team.*** Have parishioners sign up to become a prayer partner, a secret intercessor who promises to pray for a particular catechumen or candidate throughout the RCIA process.

Traits of an Effective RCIA Sponsor

There is no one way to be a good sponsor, but certain qualities do increase a sponsor's potential. These qualities will help you recruit, maintain, and even *be* a better sponsor:

- ***A sponsor is willing to share the faith.*** A sponsor should talk with his or her catechumen about his or her faith, love, commitment, and relationship with Jesus Christ. This person shares simple ways to put our faith into words and actions to help the catechumen deepen his or her relationship with Jesus.
- ***A sponsor is prayerful.*** A sponsor has and knows the importance of an active prayer life and prays for his or her catechumen. This person is aware of and sensitive to the many different ways of praying. He or she may even teach the catechumen how to pray.

- ***A sponsor is welcoming and hospitable.*** A good sponsor makes his or her catechumen feel comfortable in and around the parish. Whether at an RCIA session, Mass, or another parish function, this person goes out of the way to greet the catechumen, sit and visit with him or her, and introduce him or her to others.

- ***A sponsor is a good listener.*** All catechumens are seeking God in one way or another. Some are very forthcoming with their story and questions; others are more reluctant. Sometimes what is *not* said is just as revealing. A good sponsor remains available, respects privacy, and listens as much (if not more) than he or she talks.

- ***A sponsor is understanding and supportive.*** A sponsor tries to understand the catechumen's feelings, concerns, joys, and uncertainties. This person shows empathy and compassion no matter what is going on and how the person feels. If something serious arises, he or she can refer the catechumen to the RCIA coordinator or pastor.

- ***A sponsor is informed and involved.*** Good sponsors help their catechumen by staying informed of news and events not only in the parish and the RCIA but also in the larger and universal Church. This person reads the bulletin, follows the Church in the media, and keeps track of the RCIA schedule. Better yet, he or she attends every session possible and obtains copies of the material to share in the experience and renew his or her own understanding.

- ***A sponsor is willing to challenge.*** If a catechumen shows a lack of commitment, serious hesitation, or resistance to the process, the sponsor should ask kindly about the situation. Being honest and willing to talk about potential conflicts will ensure the spiritual well-being and best interests of the catechumen and the Church. The RCIA coordinator or pastor may know the best way to address difficult situations.

Integrating the Parish Community

The RCIA process can renew the entire parish. It is a constant reminder of our roots, our heritage, and our traditions. Each beginning offers an opportunity for all to revisit their own journey of faith, to share how God is with us, and to mature in our relationships with God and each other. When expressed through the life of the parish, the RCIA can facilitate a continuous conversion process throughout the community and an ever clearer image of the reign of God.

- Provide RCIA updates for the parish bulletin, newsletter, or website, sharing ways parishioners can help the group and introducing them to the names and faces of the participants (see also hospitality and intercessory teams).

- Post the names of catechumens and candidates in the adoration chapel to remind visitors to intercede for RCIA participants.

- As you approach the rite of election, post photos of the RCIA participants in the vestibule or narthex of church to remind the parish to welcome and pray for the group.

- Invite parish groups and committees to send an encouraging letter to the group. These could include an introduction to their membership or ministry as well as a special gift:

    - A men's or women's group might provide journals or writing utensils.

    - The rosary group might send rosaries for the lesson on Catholic prayers and practices.

    - The fish friers or food-pantry volunteers might provide snacks for each session.

    - The altar guild or maintenance crew might deliver flowers for the room each month.

Discerning Individual Needs

No one can predict the makeup of an RCIA group. The variety of ages, backgrounds, and catechetical needs within any group, year, or parish can be huge.

Religious Heritage and Formation Level

Participants will come to you from a variety of faith backgrounds. Some may have had no faith formation or have little, if any, concept of Church, faith, and salvation. Others may have inherited biases against certain Church teachings. You may have someone who was baptized and active in another Christian denomination and someone who was baptized Catholic but not raised in the Church.

While catechumens and candidates can usually participate in the sessions together, the lived experiences of an active Christian and an unbaptized or uncatechized adult make for very different perspectives. In the celebration of the rites, the reality of baptism must be evidenced, so during the rites these two groups may need to be separated as a way of addressing their separate needs and backgrounds. Effective entrance questions and strong communications among the RCIA leaders, sponsors, and pastor should prevent critical surprises and lead each participant to initiation or full reception into the universal Church.

Be careful not to generate a one-size-fits-all process. As you prepare for each session, cater the discussions, questions, and activities to each group's needs. If you anticipate a strong interest in a subject or benefit to highlighting certain aspects of Catholic teaching or practice, do so with prudence, charity, and guidance from your pastor.

Personal Commitments and Situations

While many adults come to the RCIA process with a strong internal desire to learn about the Catholic faith, others may participate out of insistence from their parents or other outside sources. Some struggle to accept the process amid current lifestyle choices or objections to Christian moral teaching and social justice. Others may face obstacles to regular attendance or full participation—variable part-time work schedules, an overabundance of extracurriculars or schoolwork, limited access to transportation, or medical or physical challenges. Here your loving response is essential in guiding each participant in his or her faith journey.

Each participant has human dignity and is created in the image of God. Most of us have been affected by sin, whether our own or that of others, but all of us are called to conversion and new life. Use the RCIA process and other parish resources to provide the time, support, and environment each participant requires.

Sacramental Status

Establish each individual's sacramental status early on—both for baptism and for marriage. For those in need of annulments, involve the pastor as soon as possible; he will determine their specific needs, explain the necessary steps, and begin the process with them. Reassure them that the Church embraces *all* children—whether from valid or invalid marriages or conceived outside of marriage—as precious gifts from God. If older children are in need of Christian initiation, proceed as normal with the support of catechists and parents. If there are any concerns about a participant's sacramental status, refer that participant to your parish priest.

How to Use Journey of Faith

Journey of Faith consists of:

- *Forty-eight* catechetical lessons
- *Three Leader Guides*: Inquiry, Catechumenate, and Enlightenment and Mystagogy
- Three volumes of *The Word Into Life*: one for each of the Sunday cycles (Years A, B, and C)

Catechetical Lessons (Handouts)

Journey of Faith is presented in forty-eight personal, engaging, and manageable lessons so that uncatechized or nominally catechized teens can hear the good news. The lessons are divided according to the four periods of initiation:

- Sixteen ***Inquiry*** (Q#) lessons broadly cover basic questions in areas such as: what is faith, revelation, prayer, the Bible, and the meaning of the Mass and Catholic practices.
- Sixteen ***Catechumenate*** (C#) lessons address more catechetical aspects of our faith: the Church, the sacraments, the moral life, and so forth.
- Eight ***Enlightenment*** (E#) lessons focus on preparing the elect for the various rites, especially the sacraments of initiation, and guide them through Lenten themes and events.
- Eight ***Mystagogy*** (M#) lessons redirect the focus of new Catholics from learning to living.

In each lesson you will find:

- "In Short": a brief list of statements outlining the main ideas
- an explanation of a faith topic
- related Scripture and *Catechism* references
- quotes and reflections from Church documents, Catholic writings, and the saints
- questions for reflection and discussion
- a journaling prompt and/or activity that applies the concepts and engages participants
- integrated images, icons, and sidebars throughout the program.

The tables of contents and following schedules provide an effective and logical order for a typical parish-based RCIA process. You can also follow the themes of the *Lectionary* readings, supporting them with these handouts as indicated in *The Word Into Life* (see below). Because the topics and themes are closely connected and recur throughout the *Journey of Faith* program and liturgical year, the handouts and *Leader Guides* can serve as ongoing tools. We understand that time is limited and that questions and issues arise. Ultimately, how you use the material depends on you, your parish, and the needs of each participant.

Distributing the handout prior to the session allows participants to reflect on the topic and respond to the questions ahead of time. Both the handouts and the *Leader Guides* are designed to walk you through the sessions and facilitate discussions, highlighting and reinforcing essential points along the way.

Leader Guides

To help you present each topic and prepare for the sessions, each *Journey of Faith Leader Guide* provides a lesson plan for each catechetical handout within its respective period and an alphabetical glossary of terms contained in those lessons. When used sequentially as a set, this creates a comprehensive RCIA program that is adaptable to any parish and group of participants. Along with the schedules and supply lists in this *Inquiry Leader Guide*, *Journey of Faith* equips RCIA leaders to engage participants and their sponsors in the process of conversion and faith formation.

Each lesson plan is designed to fill a ninety-minute session, not including any liturgical celebrations. As session times may vary, the material in each lesson plan can be adapted to your specific needs. Continuously assess your participants' understanding and tailor your presentation to what the group needs.

In addition to the complete participant lesson, leaders will find instructions, background information, notes, and more under these headings:

Catechism	sections of the *Catechism of the Catholic Church* covered by that lesson, and a key quote selected from the list.
Objectives	learning goals; what participants should know and be able to do after the session.
Leader Meditation	brief reflections, questions, and prayers on a Scripture passage related to the lesson's topic (see information at right).
Related *Catholic Updates*	suggested issues of the parish newsletter from Liguori Publications that explores Catholic teaching and tradition. Supplementing the handout with these articles, especially if shared with the parish congregation, promotes greater understanding by all the faithful.
Leader Preparation	tips and reminders to guide the presenter's preparation for the session, including a list of that lesson's vocabulary and special supplies.
Welcome	reminders and ideas for the beginning of a session, whether transitioning from a Liturgy of the Word or settling the group in.
Opening Scripture	a reading from Scripture that sets the context and supports the lesson's topic and discussion.
Discussion of Lesson Handout	points, prompts, suggested responses, and additional references for the leader, organized by section.
Journaling and/or **Activity**	instructions and reminders for the journaling prompt(s) and/or a summative activity.
Closing Prayer	prompts or texts to end the session in prayer.
Take-home or **Looking Ahead**	exercises that participants complete between sessions to deepen and apply their formation. Leaders should instruct participants prior to each departure and follow up as needed.

Preparing With Scripture

Before each session, catechists and team members should read the Scripture passage for that lesson as well as review the lesson plan and any accompanying catechetical material. As you reflect on the passage, consider these questions:

- Become part of the narrative. What stories of your own faith journey come to mind?
- What questions are raised in your mind?
- What are the sights, sounds, and feelings that emerge?
- What are the names and stories of the key individuals?
- What are the connections, if any, between the passage and the lesson's topic? Between the passage and other Bible readings, especially those for Sunday Mass?
- How does this passage apply to today's Church and Christian living?
- If you have time, read a devotion or commentary on the passage to deepen your understanding.

If needed, adjust the session's timing or focus to maximize your catechumens' and candidates' success with the material. After your lesson is set, relax and enjoy the opportunity to share your faith with those who are eager to be touched by God's Spirit.

The Word Into Life

The liturgy is fundamental to the RCIA process, and *The Word Into Life* allows you to connect the Sunday Mass readings to the *Journey of Faith* program. This deepens the process' connection to the Church year and respects the natural rhythm of the call to conversion.

Each volume of *The Word Into Life* contains:

- the *Lectionary* texts for every Sunday and holy day of obligation within that cycle
- commentaries and questions on the readings for leaders and participants
- cross-references to every catechetical lesson in *Journey of Faith*

As a main resource, *The Word Into Life* is most effective when used for an entire liturgical year. If your program's schedule is shorter or crosses between two or more Sunday cycles, make sure each team member and catechist has a copy of each volume needed and all forty-eight *Journey of Faith* lessons are covered in an appropriate manner.

Catholic Update and More

Liguori Publications offers many resources for RCIA leaders and participants, including DVDs, pamphlets, and electronic publications. *Catholic Update* newsletters explore Catholic teaching and tradition in easy to understand language. Because they often address the sacraments and topics of interest to an adult RCIA audience, suggested *Catholic Update* newsletters are included in each lesson plan. Always explain the purpose of any supplemental material and leave time in the sessions to share reactions and findings.

Visit Liguori.org for our full and latest offerings and ordering details. Be sure to purchase copies well in advance of the scheduled sessions. Ordering enough for the entire parish builds a community connection to the RCIA and a foundation for ongoing catechesis.

No matter how far in advance you plan your purchase, unexpected things come up. Whether it's a new volunteer to your RCIA team or a new family of participants, these last-minute changes can leave you in a bind. You know photocopying material is a violation of the copyright, but what do you do when you only have a few days (or hours) to find a solution?

You may not know that Liguori can help you out in these kinds of emergencies through rush delivery or even short-term permission to duplicate material while you wait for your order to arrive. Please call us at 1-800-325-9521 or email us at Liguori@Liguori.org to find out how we can help.

Practical Suggestions

Materials and Supplies

The leader preparation tips suggest helpful items specific to each lesson. For most sessions, you will need the following:

- a complete set of *Journey of Faith* handouts for each participant (It's best to buy additional sets for sponsors.)
- copies of the *Journey of Faith Leader Guides* for each catechist and team member
- copies of *The Word Into Life* for each catechist and team member (optional but recommended)
- multiple, ideally individual, copies of the Holy Bible (*Journey of Faith* uses the *New American Bible,* revised edition.)
- multiple, ideally individual, copies of the *Catechism of the Catholic Church (CCC)*
- a Bible concordance to help leaders locate related passages (optional)
- a simple white candle in a secure holder
- matches or a lighter
- nametags for the first few sessions
- comfortable seating for each individual positioned near tables or other writing/ working surfaces
- pens, pencils, and notebooks or paper (see Journaling and Notes sidebar)

Journaling and Notes

Like the faith journey, the reflection and writing process can be highly personal. Some write more than others or prefer certain mediums and styles. The handouts offer limited writing space for questions, Bible references, and activities. However, keeping an RCIA journal fulfills a number of purposes:

- recalling thoughts and reactions to the topics, readings, and discussions
- writing longer responses to the questions and activities
- jotting down notes and questions during and beyond the sessions
- recording insights, ideas, and feelings throughout the RCIA process

At the first session, provide all participants with a journal, or, if they prefer, they may bring their own. Encourage them to use it every week and to spend time in personal reflection. Let them know they are not required to share anything private with the group or with their sponsor.

Preparing a Sacred Space

Scripture reading, faith discussions, and prayer require reverence. Your environment sets the tone for each session and much of the process. Make sure the room has an inviting atmosphere. Modifying the space to match the session's topic, RCIA period, or liturgical season will assist the participants as they move through the process and grow in their familiarity with Catholic culture, ethos, and identity. You may also want to pray with the group for the Holy Spirit to be with you as you begin your opening Scripture each session to better prepare the hearts and minds of participants and yourself as a leader.

- Reverently lay the Bible or *Lectionary* next to the candle. During each of the sacred seasons, place liturgically colored fabric underneath: green during Ordinary Time, violet during Advent and Lent, and white during Christmas and Easter.
- Add religious images and objects to the space.
- Appeal to all of the participants' senses. Consider playing sacred music as they enter the space or meditative sounds as they pray or write in their journals. Encourage anyone who provides refreshments to be creative and to match the snack to the topic, season, or a saint whose feast lands on or near the session date.

In the Beginning: The First Few Sessions

1. Warmly welcome the participants, sponsors, and guests. Encourage sponsors to attend every session with their participant.
2. Have each person introduce himself or herself. Ask each one to briefly explain what led him or her to inquire about the Catholic faith or accept a supporting role in the RCIA. Encourage people to share information about their family and faith backgrounds.
3. Distribute the materials, state your expectations for the program, and give any instructions or announcements, such as directions to the restrooms.
4. Explain the purpose and meaning of the sessions. Uncatechized adults may not be familiar with prayer, candlelighting, Scripture reading and reflection, faith sharing, or religious instruction—especially in a Catholic setting.
5. Whenever reading from Scripture, make sure the reader is comfortable with reading aloud and understands the passage. Scripture should be proclaimed prayerfully and clearly and, if possible, with prior preparation. Never oblige anyone, but invite all interested to receive guidance from a practiced leader or minister.
6. Always model the behavior and etiquette desired, whether at Mass or in the sessions. While gentle reminders are needed at times, people of all ages learn from example.
7. Allow time before, after, or outside the sessions for fellowship, socializing, and refreshments. This allows the personal connections and private conversations essential to spiritual growth to take place.

Answering Questions

Most participants enter the RCIA process with religious or spiritual questions as well as preconceived notions of the Catholic Church.
More questions will undoubtedly emerge as they near initiation. Furthermore, the time they spend in the sessions and even with the parish community will not completely encompass their experience and knowledge of faith. Catechists and team members must be willing to engage tough questions and events in order to further the individual's understanding and conversion.

Always respect every question and respond to it as adequately as you can, especially if it is pertinent to the topic and the entire group. Never attempt to answer a question that goes beyond your knowledge or expertise.

If you don't feel qualified or aren't sure how to answer:

- Let the person know you need time to prepare a proper or fuller answer. Offer to respond at the next session or outside of the sessions, and follow through.
- Check trusted and authoritative sources for relevant Church teachings and key factors in your response. Share your references or recommend similar material when the question is revisited.
- Consult with your director or coordinator of religious education, pastor, or diocesan official, or set up a private conversation between that contact and the person to answer the question more thoroughly.

If an individual query or a barrage of questions draw the discussion away from the topic at hand, consider dedicating a portion or an entire session to the subject of interest.

RCIA Schedules Using *Journey of Faith*

Program or Academic Year
(Fall-Pentecost)

The following guidelines direct parishes in scheduling an RCIA program lasting eight to nine months each year. Weekly schedules may vary from year to year depending on when Advent, Lent, and the rites occur. Merging or separating lessons into adjacent weeks will keep you on track and maximize the program's connection to liturgical feasts and themes.

Journey of Faith strongly recommends continuing after Easter into a discrete period of mystagogy. This provides the parish an additional opportunity to join the neophytes and witness to the value of, and universal call to, ongoing faith formation.

Three Months Before Advent (August-September)		
First Week	Q1	"Welcome to the RCIA!"
Second Week	Q2	"What Is Faith?"
Third Week	Q3	"The Holy Trinity"
Fourth Week	Q4	"Who Is Jesus Christ?"

Two Months Before Advent (September-October)		
First Week	Q5	"The Bible"
	Q6	"Divine Revelation"
Second Week	Q7	"Your Prayer Life"
	Q8	"Catholic Prayers and Practices"
Third Week	Q9	"The Mass"
	C5	"The Sacrament of the Eucharist"
Fourth Week	Q10	"The Church Year"
	Q11	"Places in a Catholic Church"

One Month Before Advent (October-November)		
First Week	Q12	"Who Shepherds the Church?"
	Q13	"The Church as Community"
Second Week	Q14	"Mary"
	Q15	"The Saints"
Third Week	Q16	"Eschatology: The 'Last Things'"
Fourth Week/ Christ the King	C1	"The RCIA Process and Rites" (*anticipates rites of acceptance and welcoming*)

Advent and Christmas (November-December)		
First Week	C10	"The People of God"
Second Week	C11	"The Early Church"
	C12	"Church History"
Third Week	C2	"The Sacraments: An Introduction"
Fourth Week/ Christmas		BREAK
Holy Family/ Epiphany	C8	"The Sacrament of Matrimony"
	C9	"The Sacrament of Holy Orders"
Baptism of the Lord (OT)	C3	"The Sacrament of Baptism"
	C4	"The Sacrament of Confirmation"

One Month Before Lent (January-February)		
First Week	C6	"The Sacrament of Penance and Reconciliation"
	C7	"The Sacrament of Anointing of the Sick"
Second Week	C13	"Christian Moral Living"
	C14	"The Dignity of Life"
Third Week	C15	"A Consistent Ethic of Life"
	C16	"Social Justice"
Week of Ash Wednesday	E1	Election: Saying "Yes" to Jesus (anticipates rite of election)

Lent/Enlightenment (February-March)		
First Week	E2	"Living Lent"
Second Week	E3	"Scrutinies:..."
	E4	"The Creed" (*anticipates third Sunday*)
Third Week	E5	"The Way of the Cross"
Fourth Week	E6	"The Lord's Prayer" (*anticipates fifth Sunday*)
Fifth Week	E7	"The Meaning of Holy Week"
Holy Week	E8	Easter Vigil Retreat

Easter/Mystagogy (April-May)		
First Week		BREAK (or appropriate fellowship)
Second Week	M1	"Conversion: A Lifelong Process"
Third Week	M2	"The Role of the Laity"
	M7	"Family Life"
Fourth Week	M3	"Your Spiritual Gifts"
Fifth Week	M4	"Discernment"
Sixth Week/ Ascension	M5	"Our Call to Holiness"
	M6	"Living the Virtues"
Seventh Week/ Pentecost *(Final Session)*	M8	"Evangelization"

Calendar Year (ongoing, sequential)

The forty-eight *Journey of Faith* lessons can be followed sequentially with only minor adjustments for the rites and the Lenten season. Using this model, parishes would begin about *four weeks after Pentecost*. To complete the calendar year, we recommend a single-week break for Christmas and Easter and a two-week break shortly after Pentecost for program renewal, training, and family time. Refer to the *Journey of Faith* lessons listed in My RCIA Schedule.

Liturgical Year (ongoing, nonsequential)

For parishes following the ongoing catechumenal model, each period in the RCIA process is available all year long. We recommend using separate but simultaneous tracks for inquiry and catechumenate and a third track during Lent and Easter. In this way, the process is open and flexible enough to support and honor the needs and pace of each catechumen and candidate.

In this model, most individuals will spend a year or more in the RCIA process. The lessons will be used as they relate to the themes of each Sunday's readings. All forty-eight lessons are applied within each volume of *The Word Into Life*, so no matter when you start, a year-long formation will nearly guarantee a complete exploration of the topics in the program. Any gaps can be incorporated into the individual's process if time is a factor and doing so is prudent.

My RCIA Schedule

This chart can be reused or adjusted each year according to your parish's RCIA calendar. It is also valuable for participants who may be on a separate path from the rest of the group. Make sure to record all key dates and details and to follow your RCIA director's or pastor's instructions.

Parish: ______________________

Pastor/RCIA Director: ______________________

Catechist(s)/
Team Member(s): ______________________

Participant(s): ______________________

Class Time(s): ______________________

Class Location: ______________________

Mass Time: ______________________

Easter Vigil: ______________________

INQUIRY

Lesson Title	Session Date	Lesson Title	Session Date
Q1: Welcome to the RCIA!		Q9: The Mass	
Q2: What is Faith?		Q10: The Church Year	
Q3: The Holy Trinity		Q11: Places in a Catholic Church	
Q4: Who is Jesus Christ?		Q12: Who Shepherds the Church?	
Q5: The Bible		Q13: The Church as Community	
Q6: Divine Revelation		Q14: Mary	
Q7: Your Prayer Life		Q15: The Saints	
Q8: Catholic Prayers and Practices		Q16: Eschatology: the "Last Things"	

CATECHUMENATE

Lesson Title	Session Date	Lesson Title	Session Date
C1: The RCIA Process and Rites		C9: The Sacrament of Holy Orders	
C2: The Sacraments: An Introduction		C10: The People of God	
C3: The Sacrament of Baptism		C11: The Early Church	
C4: The Sacrament of Confirmation		C12: Church History	
C5: The Sacrament of the Eucharist		C13: Christian Moral Living	
C6: The Sacrament of Penance and Reconciliation		C14: The Dignity of Life	
C7: The Sacrament of Anointing of the Sick		C15: A Consistent Ethic of Life	
C8: The Sacrament of Matrimony		C16: Social Justice	

ENLIGHTENMENT

Lesson Title	Session Date
E1: Election: Saying "Yes" to Jesus	
E2: Living Lent	
E3: Scrutinies: Looking Within	
E4: The Creed	
E5: The Way of the Cross	
E6: The Lord's Prayer	
E7: The Meaning of Holy Week	
E8: Easter Vigil Retreat	

MYSTAGOGY

Lesson Title	Session Date
M1: Conversion: A Lifelong Process	
M2: The Role of the Laity	
M3: Your Spiritual Gifts	
M4: Discernment	
M5: Our Call to Holiness	
M6: Living the Virtues	
M7: Family Life	
M8: Evangelization	

Q1: Welcome to the RCIA

Objectives

Participants will…

- recognize the RCIA as an opportunity to ask questions about God, faith, and the Catholic Church.
- recall the origin and periods of the RCIA process.
- interpret the RCIA as Jesus' invitation to join the Church.

Leader Meditation

Psalm 139:1–16

Reflect on your faith journey—if possible, before the Blessed Sacrament—considering the many times God has protected and guided you. He has brought you to this moment and has led and entrusted each inquirer to your care. Ponder this great trust, this opportunity to be their companion and guide. Pray for wisdom and courage. Rely on the Lord's help. He will lead you as you lead them.

Related *Catholic Updates*

- "What It Means to Be Catholic: Satisfying 12 Human Needs" (C0708A)
- "What Catholics Believe: An Overview of Catholic Teaching" (C8610A)

Leader Preparation

- Read the lesson handout, this lesson plan, the opening Scripture passage, and the *Catechism* sections.
- Read the front sections of this leader guide. The USCCB website may also help you explain the RCIA and *Catechism* further.
- Be familiar with the vocabulary terms in this lesson: RCIA, rites, catechist, inquiry, catechumen(ate), godparent, sponsor, purification and enlightenment, sacraments of initiation, mystagogy, catechism. Definitions can be found in this guide's glossary.
- Obtain copies of the *New American Bible* (or other Catholic translation) and *Catechism* for each participant as well as any required materials listed earlier in this guide on page 15. Enlist creative ways to supply prayer journals and other unique items (see activity below and "Integrating the Parish Community" above).
- Gather copies of your parish's RCIA calendar or a list of key event dates for each participant.

Welcome

As the group gathers, welcome each individual, repeating back names. Direct participants to the supplies, nametags, refreshments, and restrooms. Take some time for introductions. (The activity at the end of the lesson is a good ice breaker that can be used at the beginning or the end of the session.) After giving initial instructions and announcements, take questions and respond briefly. Begin promptly.

Opening Scripture

Psalm 139:1–16

Read the passage aloud from a Catholic Bible or study *Lectionary*. Allow for a moment of silence, and then ask for comments or reactions to the words. Finally, share a few words of encouragement and affirmation. Indicate that God is leading them and has been with them their whole lives.

Light the candle and explain that it is a sign and reminder of the Lord's presence. Jesus said, "I am the light of the world" and "where two or three are gathered together in my name, there am I in the midst of them" (John 8:12 and 9:5; Matthew 18:20). Begin with this prayer:

Heavenly Father, through the gift of your Son and the power of your Holy Spirit, we ask you to guide us in our faith journey. Help us to hear your voice and to follow where you lead. And give us your peace. Amen.

> "God…reveals himself and gives himself to man, at the same time bringing man a superabundant light as he searches for the ultimate meaning of his life."
>
> CCC 26

Q1 INQUIRY

In Short:

- Jesus invites you to the Church.
- The RCIA is a time to ask questions.
- The RCIA process has four periods.

Welcome to the RCIA

There are many people searching for a way to meet their spiritual needs and identify with a community of faith. People who feel the desire to know more about the Catholic Church and to explore its life may simply need a friendly invitation. Perhaps your spouse or a close friend is Catholic, or you saw or read something that prompted questions and inspired interest. The Rite of Christian Initiation of Adults is the Church's way of extending an invitation.

Take Your Time

No need to rush; it makes sense to go at your own pace and move thoughtfully through the biggest decisions of our lives. People rarely get married, buy a house, change careers, or move cities without giving such significant decisions appropriate time and consideration. Our initial interest leads to further exploration, helping us get to know our options and ourselves better. You might have felt this tug at your soul before and have only now chosen to act upon it.

Our Catholic faith isn't so much a set of beliefs, although we do have them, but more of a relationship that starts with our Lord and develops as we observe and encounter him in our lives.

Feelings can be powerful, but you wouldn't want a relationship founded only on feelings. Relationships are stronger and healthier when they're built on solid ground. We trust and respect decisions that are well-considered, shared, and entered into freely.

- *How do you make big decisions?*
- *Why are you interested in learning more about the Catholic Church?*

What Does the RCIA Mean?

The RCIA stands for the **Rite of Christian Initiation of Adults**. It's the process through which unbaptized adults and older children are formed in the teachings and practices of Catholicism and are *initiated* into the Catholic Church. It's marked by various **rites** or rituals, which usually occur at Sunday Mass. Sometimes the process includes baptized adult Christians or Catholics who are preparing to receive the sacraments of confirmation and Eucharist.

Why Do Catholics Initiate Others Into Their Faith?

Jesus told his followers to "make disciples of all nations" (Matthew 28:19). No other ancient religion sought converts: not Egyptians, Greeks, or Romans. But Christians—not just Catholics—still welcome and invite anyone to join us.

ADULTS

Before moving forward with your lesson, ask if any inquirer is unfamiliar with the Bible. Briefly review its organization before you begin (see *Q5: The Bible*). Distinguish between the Old and New Testaments but emphasize the importance of each and their unity as the inspired word of God. The Old Testament, or Hebrew Scriptures, covers the beginning of salvation history within and through the Hebrews' (or Israelites') covenant relationship with God. The New Testament covers the fulfillment of salvation history in and through Jesus' life, death, and resurrection and includes teachings and letters from the early Christian Church.

Welcome to the RCIA

Start the discussion with general questions about what brought everyone to the group today. Such as:

- Is anyone here with a family member or friend?
- Do you know a parishioner here?
- How were you introduced to the Catholic faith and our RCIA process?

Take Your Time

Read the questions in the lesson together and invite participants to respond to each one. This will deepen the group's knowledge of each other's backgrounds and perspectives. It will also help the team members and sponsors to form a sense of each participant's needs.

Jesus Says, "Come!"

As you read through the Bible passages, help participants understand Jesus' message to us.

Jesus doesn't just want us to follow him into the faith blindly. He wants us to make the choice freely and with all the information we need to make a decision.

Is the RCIA New?

Invite participants to ask any questions they may have so far about the process. Acknowledge each one and thank the inquirer or candidate for his or her openness. Address any issue you can simply and immediately. Assure participants that future lessons will cover most topics and answer their questions in greater depth.

Review the history and purpose of the RCIA. Emphasize that participants do not need to become experts in doctrine or prayer. Rather, they will receive instruction on basic teachings and beliefs and guided practice in various spiritual activities, including the rites.

How Long Does the RCIA Last?

Distribute copies of your RCIA calendar and point out key dates and milestones. Encourage participants to enter each session and event into their personal calendar(s).

This is because we believe that:

- Following Jesus makes people happier and more at peace, both here and in the life to come. We believe the Catholic Church has the fullest and most authentic understanding of Jesus.
- The Christian community is strengthened by the conversion of all people, who are created in God's likeness and called to discipleship.

"I came so that they might have life and have it more abundantly."

John 10:10

"I have told you this so that my joy may be in you and your joy may be complete."

John 15:11

Jesus Says, "Come!"

Jesus doesn't just want us to follow him into the faith blindly. He wants us to make the choice freely and with all the information we need to make a decision.

- "Come, and you will see" (John 1:39). Jesus invites people to observe him to see if he accomplishes what he says. You will study Jesus closely in the RCIA.
- "Come after me" (Matthew 4:19). These are some of the first words Jesus spoke during his ministry. He didn't say, "Understand me" or, "Obey me." He allowed people to consider his ways and to freely make up their minds.
- "Come, follow me" (Mark 10:21; Luke 18:22). "Follow me" is perhaps the simplest definition of our faith. The RCIA is like a winding road: hard to see far down, but revealed as you go. Fortunately, Jesus leads the way.

What Happens in the RCIA?

Most processes are a series of weekly sessions with a team of **catechists** (religion teachers), sponsors, and fellow participants. Each session is a safe place to discuss the faith and explore questions about Catholicism or religion and spirituality in general. All questions are welcome and honored.

God invited Mary to be the mother of Jesus because Jesus couldn't be born without her free and informed consent. Before giving her consent, Mary asked "How can this be?" (Luke 1:34). Like Mary, we all have free will to accept Jesus into our lives and to ask our questions. That's how much God respects—and even expects—your honest questions.

Is the RCIA New?

This process began in the earliest years of the Church. In those first centuries, it was a challenge to convert to Christianity because the Roman Empire often persecuted those who didn't follow its pagan religion. The Church wanted to make sure that candidates really knew what they were doing and were willing to stand up for their faith in a hostile environment. In the 1960s, the Church called for a return to this early model in order to provide Christian formation in the same gradual way people experience and enter any lasting and loving relationship.

- *What questions do you have today?*

How Long Does the RCIA Last?

It depends. People come with their own unique stories and needs. While many classes begin in late summer or early fall and end at Pentecost, some schedules will vary or run year-round, allowing you to proceed at your own pace.

Understanding faith is as important as having faith, and that takes time. Come with an open heart and an open mind. Get to know as much as you can. Each week, you'll be invited to reflect on Christ's words and deeds and witness or even practice some Catholic behaviors to see if you feel called to this life.

The Periods of the RCIA

1. **Inquiry** (*Evangelization and Precatechumenate*): During this period, anyone can test the waters and ask questions about the Catholic faith. No commitments or promises are made. This period can last as long as you desire—a few months up to a few years.
2. **Catechumenate**: This word comes from ancient Greek, the language of the early Church. Catechumen means "a person receiving instruction." During this period, you will study and discuss most of the Church's main beliefs. You will also have a **godparent** or **sponsor** join you on your journey. This person can be a Catholic family member, a wise and good friend, or someone from the parish suggested by the team. Your sponsor should attend the RCIA sessions with you regularly and continue conversations with you outside the RCIA. They also serve as your representative and advocate to the Church.
3. **Purification and Enlightenment** (*Lent*): This period occurs during the weeks before Easter and may include any of several optional rites. This time is more prayerful than instructional. It is a time of deeper spiritual preparation for the sacraments. Then, on the night before Easter, during the Vigil Mass on Holy Saturday, those who have completed their preparation enter the Church through the **sacraments of initiation**: baptism, confirmation, and Eucharist.
4. **Mystagogy** (*Postbaptismal Catechesis*): This final period usually lasts several weeks—from Easter to Pentecost. It's a time to reflect on the mysteries of the sacraments and to begin living out your new faith in practical ways.

Why Should I Attend Mass and Participate in Parish Events?

The Church celebrates the Mass because Jesus invites us to "do this in memory of me" (Luke 22:19). In worship, prayer, and holy Communion, Catholics are united with God and each other. That togetherness also reveals the Lord: "Where two or three are gathered together in my name, there am I in the midst of them" (Matthew 18:20).

While we can—and should—pray and study alone, God wants us to experience his love as part of a community. Faith is both private and public, and—as in any loving relationship—God doesn't want you to walk alone or keep your feelings to yourself. Publicly expressing and receiving love together makes it stronger, more real, and inspires others. So when the parish sees and hears your journey—and you witness members' ongoing and growing faith—you strengthen each other along the way.

- *Name a Catholic you admire. What do you admire about him or her?*

How Do I Start?

- **Be openhearted:** Come eager to learn.
- **Ask questions:** Be ready to address and explore your concerns.
- **Talk to wise mentors:** Let your understanding grow as you discuss ideas with trusted friends.
- **Pray for wisdom:** Ask Jesus for what you need to follow him.
- **Read the *Catechism of the Catholic Church (CCC)*:** A **catechism** is a summary of religious teachings for the purpose of instruction. Consider this a great asset for your journey.
- **Keep a journal:** Let it be a place to record and respond to questions or comments and to reflect on your journey and growth in writing and prayer.

The Periods of the RCIA

Discuss each period, providing parish or diocesan details to convey expectations and schedules. Point out that the rites and process will be discussed further in lesson C1.

Remind participants that although each individual—not the Church—decides when to take the next step, the enlightenment and mystagogy periods almost always occur during Lent and Easter respectively, given the Church's mandate to celebrate initiation at the Easter Vigil.

How Do I Start?

Introduce participants to the *Catechism*. Be aware that some may find it intimidating. It is lengthy. Some coming from other Christian faith heritages may assume it contains teachings that are contrary to the Bible. They may need to be reassured that the *Catechism* is consistent with the teachings of the Bible and filled with many quotes from sacred Scripture, along with quotes by saints and fundamental teachings of the Christian faith. (The USCCB website may be a helpful resource as you prepare an explanation about what the *Catechism* is.)

Emphasize the importance of keeping a prayer journal. If you haven't distributed any provided journals, do so now. Encourage participants to use theirs as a travelogue of their faith journey and record of their growing relationship with Christ.

Remind them they will not have to share anything they consider private.

Consider writing the facts on sticky notes or index cards. Include the team members and sponsors, too. The facts can be generic or specific, religious or not.

INQUIRY

JOURNEY OF FAITH

Write three facts about yourself on a slip of paper. Place them in a pile with all the others. As your leader reads each one, guess who the fact belongs to.

Journey of Faith for Adults: Inquiry, Q1 (826252)
Imprimi Potest: Stephen T. Rehrauer, CSsR, Provincial, Denver Province, the Redemptorists.

Imprimatur: "In accordance with CIC 827, permission to publish has been granted on March 7, 2016, by the Most Reverend Edward M. Rice, Auxiliary Bishop, Archdiocese of St. Louis. Permission to publish is an indication that nothing contrary to Church teaching is contained in this work. It does not imply any endorsement of the opinions expressed in the publication, nor is any liability assumed by this permission."

Contributing writer: Fr. Dave Heney. Editors of 2016 edition: Denise Bossert, Julia DiSalvo, and Joan McKamey. Design: Lorena Mitre Jimenez. Images: Shutterstock.

Compliant with *The Roman Missal, Third Edition*.

Liguori PUBLICATIONS
A Redemptorist Ministry

Printed in the United States of America
20 19 18 17 16 / 5 4 3 2 1
Third Edition

ISBN 978-0-7648-2625-2
90000>
9 780764 826252

Closing Prayer

Lord of life, you are the true shepherd. You care for us as a shepherd cares for his sheep. You lead us up and down the paths of life and guide us into the safety of the sheepfold when it is dark. You defend us with your life. Help us to recognize your voice as sheep recognize the voice of their shepherd. Guide us this week and walk with us along our paths. Amen.

Take-home

This week, let participants begin to capture their faith journey and questions in their journal. Encourage them to explore and skim their Bible(s), *Catechism*, lessons, and other materials for answers and topics of interest.

Q2: What Is Faith?

Catechism: 142–165, 302, 854

Objectives

Participants will...

- recognize faith as a free gift that builds our understanding of God's love.
- acknowledge that faith is not at odds with rational thought or science.
- identify multiple ways in which we can nurture and practice faith.

Leader Meditation

John 14:1–4

How strong is your faith? How would you define it? When you pray, do you believe God hears you? Do you trust that God is intimately involved in your life, even with its difficulties and imperfections? Most important, do you see the face of God when you are faced with questions and challenges?

Related *Catholic Updates*

- "God Is Love" (C0604A)
- "'Light of Faith': Key Themes From Pope Francis' First Encyclical" (C1310A)

Leader Preparation

- Read the lesson handout, this lesson plan, the opening Scripture passage, and the *Catechism* sections. "The Characteristics of Faith" (*CCC* 153–165) may help you to answer the participants' questions, especially those surrounding faith's relationship to science and reason.
- While the whole lesson discusses faith, the word is defined in this guide's glossary as well.
- Consider acquiring a conversion testimony or miraculous account for this session to illustrate the power of faith.
- Purchase some mustard seeds from your grocer, farmers market, or spice shop for distribution.
- Gather a list of parishioners who are willing to discuss their faith with the RCIA participants. This may include team members, potential sponsors, parish staff, and those active in ministry, prayer groups, or Bible study.
- Read Thomas Merton's famous prayer of trust from his *Thoughts in Solitude*.

Welcome

As the group gathers, welcome any new inquirers and sponsors. Check for supplies and immediate needs. Solicit questions or comments about the previous session and/or share new information and findings. Begin promptly.

Opening Scripture

John 14:1–4

Light the candle and then read the passage aloud from a Catholic Bible or study *Lectionary*. Allow for a moment of silence and then ask for any comments or reactions to the words. Build the group's awareness of our need for faith, and its power, by asking two questions: "What worries you about the Church or becoming Catholic? What inspires you and gives you hope?" Invite participants to share their responses.

> "Faith is a gift of God, a supernatural virtue infused by [God]."
> CCC 153

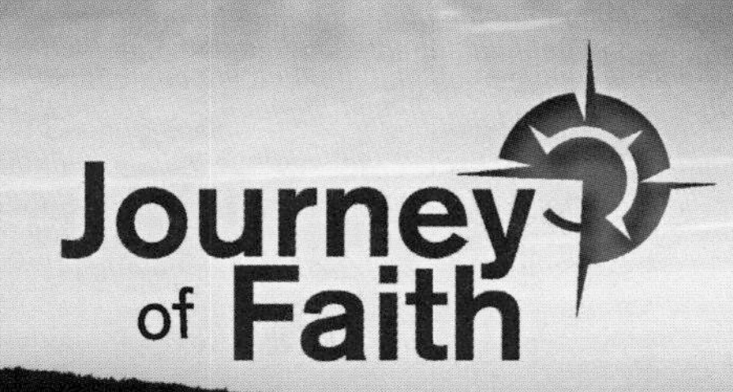

Q2 INQUIRY

In Short:

- Faith is freely given by God.
- Faith, science, and reason coexist.
- Faith grows when we nurture and share it.

- *Who or what do you have faith in?*

What Is Faith?

> "**Faith** *is the realization of what is hoped for and evidence of things not seen."*
>
> Hebrews 11:1

Faith often refers to religious belief, but we can have faith in many things. Faith begins as trust, an essential element in any healthy relationship. As young children, we believed our parents, caregivers, and teachers would provide for our needs and safety. We later extended our faith and trust to friends, classmates, romantic interests, and God.

For Catholics, the most important faith is in God as revealed through Jesus Christ. As we grow in relationship with Jesus, nurture our faith and trust in him, and come to believe in his message, our lives have greater purpose and richness. Faith is our free response to God's loving invitation.

> *"By faith, we are able to give our minds and hearts to God, to trust in his will, and to follow the direction he gives us."*
>
> *United States Catholic Catechism for Adults*, p. 37

What Does Faith Feel Like?

Spiritual longing is part of human nature (*CCC* 44). Saint Augustine wrote, "You have made us for yourself, and our hearts are restless until they rest in you" (*Confessions* 1.1).

This longing manifests itself differently in each person. For many, it arises as the search for meaning. As we ask fundamental questions—*Who am I? Where do I come from? Where am I going?*—we may be drawn into deeper reflection and tap into an inner longing for God. These questions challenge our minds, but the mind's answers are insufficient—just as, we discover, are worldly pursuits of personal fulfillment or self-improvement. We are drawn to something more.

This longing for "something more" is the beginning of our response to God's call to relationship—*friendship*—with him. Recall St. Augustine's words: "You have made us for yourself." In other words, it's built into our nature to return to God, our Creator, and to respond to his love with our lives. The *Catechism* tells us, "The desire for God is written in the human heart, because man is created by God and for God" (*CCC* 27).

ADULTS

CCC 142–165, 302, 854

What Is Faith?

Ask participants to brainstorm things they accept as real even though they don't fully understand them. *Responses may include scientific theories (evolution), psychological concepts (love), spiritual realities (angels, the resurrection), and more.*

Emphasize that this process never ends, faith is always growing, and we will never be finished with our faith formation on earth.

As you go over the reflection questions for this section, also discuss how faith in God is different from, or similar to, having faith in people or things.

What Does Faith Feel Like?

Make sure participants understand faith as a longing for God and a general trust in his existence, presence, and loving goodness. Clarify that faith is not identical to belief in specific doctrine, but in faith we continue to seek, learn, and live according to the truth.

Does Having Faith Mean We Don't Question or Doubt?

Emphasize that religious faith is not at odds with science. The truth of God cannot be "proven" in the way we prove that two plus two equals four, but our own experiences and understandings often lead us to realize that God is real.

Remind participants to trust themselves as well as God. Their presence in the RCIA is a sign of their faith.

Tell participants that although our faith contains mysteries and invisible (supernatural) realities, there are ways to confidently "know" God. This is the focus of lesson Q6, *Divine Revelation*, and some ways are hinted at in this lesson (human reason, Scripture, etc.).

Ask participants the question: "In what ways is your faith a gift?" Give an example from your own experience.

The Bible and Faith

Read the three Bible passages out loud and share their context with participants:

- Galatians 3
  In this chapter, Paul contrasts the law and works with the free gift of faith granted in Jesus Christ.
- Ephesians 2
  Like Galatians 3, Paul uses the gift of faith as proof that the Gentiles may also be reconciled to God (saved).
- Mark 9
  In this account, Jesus seems to accuse the disciples' lack of faith as a reason for their inability to heal the boy themselves.

INQUIRY

JOURNEY OF FAITH

Does this mean the way of faith is easy? That we won't ever struggle or feel far from God? Closeness to God can't be measured in terms of feelings. God is as near to us when we struggle as when we're full of peace and joy.

Faith in God is a lens through which we see all of life. We find strength in our faith in difficult times, and the joys of life are more meaningful when we recognize them as God's blessings.

> *"Although you have not seen him you love him; even though you do not see him now yet believe in him, you rejoice with an indescribable and glorious joy, as you attain the goal of [your] faith, the salvation of your souls."*
>
> 1 Peter 1:8–9

Does Having Faith Mean We Don't Question or Doubt?

Asking questions is one way we learn about the world and each other. God places questions within our hearts and minds to draw us closer to him and to his will. God also gives us perception, reason, and conscience to guide us to truth. Faith seeks understanding.

True faith isn't anti-intellectual; it makes full use of the sciences, history, logic, imagination, and emotions. The Catholic Church is so grounded in essential truth that it will support and assist you in exploring your questions. You may not always understand or like the answers, but the Church believes Christ is present in you and your journey.

> *"The believer does not seek to understand, that he may believe, but he believes that he may understand."*
>
> St. Anselm of Canterbury, *Proslogium*, chapter 1

The Bible and Faith

The Catholic understanding of faith comes largely from Scripture. The essential message of the many biblical references to faith is that it is a gift freely given by God. Christ walks with everyone who opens his or her heart to him:

> *"Through faith you are all children of God in Christ Jesus."*
>
> Galatians 3:26

> *"For by grace you have been saved through faith, and this is not from you; it is the gift of God."*
>
> Ephesians 2:8

> *"Jesus said…'Everything is possible to one who has faith.' Then the boy's father cried out, 'I do believe, help my unbelief!'"*
>
> Mark 9:23–24

- *How is participation in RCIA a sign of your growing faith?*
- *In what ways is your faith a gift? Give an example.*

What Is Faith in Action?

For most of us, our faith beginning isn't dramatic. God is like a quiet gardener who knows where the "good soil" lies within us better than we do. God plants the first small seed. But if we want our faith to grow, we have to be active about it.

Once you ask God for the gift of faith, God gives it to you freely. But we can't just ask God to give us the gift of faith and be done with it. We have to nurture the faith he gives us. We can't expect our faith in God to grow if we do nothing. Acting on faith takes practice and courage. We witness faith in action in the lives of others—and in our own choices and behaviors:

- Choosing selfless acts over personal interests
- Acting with good intentions and giving others the benefit of the doubt
- Reaching out to strangers or those with poor reputations
- Engaging in dialogue and civil discourse to determine the greater good and best solutions

Catholics claim these acts as reflections of Jesus. Jesus often said to those he healed or forgave, "Your faith has saved you." In every case, their faith was both internally felt and shown in their actions:

Luke 7:37–47
The woman who washed Jesus' feet with her tears

Matthew 8:6–8; Luke 7:2–7
The centurion who told Jesus his servant would be healed at Jesus' word

Matthew 9:20–21; Mark 5:25–28
The woman who touched Jesus' cloak

"Amen, I say to you, if you have faith the size of a mustard seed, you will say to this mountain, 'Move from here to there,' and it will move. Nothing will be impossible for you."

Matthew 17:20

As noted earlier, relying on faith can be active even in the midst of challenges. Everyone goes through times of confusion, doubt, and fear. We may fail to meet expectations or find ourselves trying to control too much. In these moments, we can lean on our faith rather than slip into discouragement or despair.

Use these steps to pray your concerns to God:

1. Quiet yourself, trusting in God's loving care. Christ patiently stands at the door of your spirit and knocks, ready to enter and remain with you (Revelation 3:20).
2. Take your problem or dilemma to God in prayer: "God, I give _______________ to you completely. Help me let go of this obstacle and trust in you."
3. Ask God to help you recognize your part, whether it was good or bad, and to conform your will to his. If a solution is presented, ask God for the strength to cooperate with it.
4. Thank God for his goodness and return to your day ready to accept whatever happens.

?

- *What can you hand over to God this week?*
- *What are your hopes and fears about this situation?*
- *What might it mean to let God manage this situation for you?*

What Is Faith in Action?

Read a passage or two from this section or divide them among a few small groups. Let each group share their answers aloud. Explain more about the meaning of each passage with the information below:

- Luke 7

(The woman who washed Jesus' feet…) Her tears testify to her remorse, as is risking her security in using costly ointment on a stranger and entering the Pharisee's home uninvited. Jesus recognizes her actions (washing, kissing), saying, "She has shown great love" (v. 47). Then he turns to her and says, "Your faith has saved you" (v. 50).

- Matthew 8, Luke 7

(healing of the centurion's servant) In both versions, the centurion makes his need known (faith in action) but demands no personal visit or miracle: "only say the word…" (8:8). Jesus responds, "Not even in Israel have I found such faith" (7:9). In Matthew, Jesus closes with, "As you have believed, let it be done for you" (8:13).

- Matthew 9, Mark 5

(The woman who touched Jesus' cloak) Her words reflect the faith behind her actions: "If only I can touch his cloak, I shall be cured" (9:21). Jesus affirms her, saying,

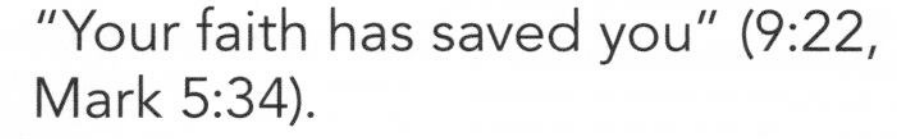

"Your faith has saved you" (9:22, Mark 5:34).

Read Matthew 17:20, which describes faith as a small seed (see also Luke 17:6). Distribute a mustard seed to each participant, then invite the group to react and share their experiences of smallness and vastness.

Lead participants through the guided prayer, pausing between steps to give them time to reflect silently on their situations and intentions. First prompt them to close their eyes, then read Revelation 3:20 or another verse out loud. To close, recite a prayer of thanks or an act of faith, then remind participants to repeat this exercise on their own as often as needed.

How Can We Nurture Our Faith?

Emphasize that faith formation is a lifelong process. No one ever reaches a point where his or her faith is "perfect" or unchanging.

Encourage participants to remain steadfast throughout the RCIA process (1 Corinthians 15:58, Philippians 1:27–30, 1 Peter 5:7–10). Active participation in Catholic parish and family life will integrate the four ways and help their faith to grow.

Share some examples of each way with participants:

- Reading: Mass (Liturgy of the Word), Bible study, *lectio divina* (prayer)
- Lifestyle: Christian morality, virtues, vocations, evangelization
- Prayer: Mass and sacraments, personal and group devotions
- Community participation: Mass and sacraments, stewardship

JOURNEY OF FAITH | INQUIRY

How Can We Nurture Our Faith?

Reading

Reading the Bible and spiritual writings of the saints or contemporary authors helps us resist temptations and inclinations to selfishness. Spiritual reading introduces us to the wisdom of others who have traveled the way of faith.

Lifestyle

Those with faith grow in God's love and share it with others. When done with faith and hope, spreading the good news of Jesus, practicing good works, and avoiding what's harmful become joys, not burdens.

> *"What good is it...if someone says he has faith but does not have works?...If a brother or sister has nothing to wear and has no food for the day, and one of you says to them, 'Go in peace, keep warm, and eat well,' but you do not give them the necessities of the body, what good is it? So also faith of itself, if it does not have works, is dead."*
>
> *James 2:14–17*

- *What does your lifestyle say about what you believe?*

Prayer

Spending time together is vital to all relationships. We grow in relationship with Jesus through speaking and listening to him in prayer.

> *"Whatever you ask for in prayer with faith, you will receive."*
>
> *Matthew 21:22*

Community Participation

The individual Christian is but one part of the body of Christ, the Church. We need to be open to the gifts God extends to us through his community. We both receive support from its wisdom and abilities and also contribute to its overall unity and strength.

Sharing your faith journey with the RCIA team, your godparent or sponsor, the parish, and the entire Church will help you experience the gift of community and build the support network we all need.

Write down any questions you have about faith, religion, and the Catholic Church. Sometime this week, approach an experienced Catholic, an RCIA team member, or a parishioner—perhaps a potential sponsor—for help in answering those questions. If a question can't be answered immediately or completely, schedule another discussion or ask for contacts and resources that may help.

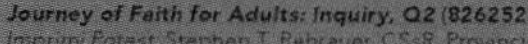

***Journey of Faith for Adults: Inquiry, Q2* (826252)**
Imprimi Potest: Stephen T. Rehrauer, CSsR, Provincial, Denver Province, the Redemptorists.
Imprimatur: "In accordance with CIC 827, permission to publish has been granted on March 7, 2016, by the Most Reverend Edward M. Rice, Auxiliary Bishop, Archdiocese of St. Louis. Permission to publish is an indication that nothing contrary to Church teaching is contained in this work. It does not imply any endorsement of the opinions expressed in the publication, nor is any liability assumed by this permission."

Contributing writer: Philip St. Romain. Editors of 2016 *Journey of Faith*: Denise Bossert, Julia DiSalvo, and Joan McKamey.
Design: Lorena Mitre Jimenez. Images: Shutterstock.

Printed in the United States of America. 20 19 18 17 16 / 5 4 3 2 1. Third Edition.

Journaling

Share the pool of parishioners to make this easier for inquirers. Distribute their names, contact information, and general availability as needed.

Closing Prayer

Read Merton's prayer of trust aloud, or recite the prayer below:

The Prayer of a Seeker

Dear God, I'm walking this road without a map in my hand. Once I knew where I was headed on this journey, but now, I'm not so sure. Anyway, all I've got are a few directions scribbled down, some advice on how to read the road signs, maybe a place up ahead to ask the way when I get lost. Help me set my feet toward you. Steer me to those who will guide me wisely. Send me true companions along the road. Teach me that feeling lost may not be cause for panic but may lead to new and challenging paths. Let me know that you are always walking with me. Amen.

Take-home

Encourage participants to continue their exploration of the materials and to reflect on their faith in God, which is nurtured and growing by their presence in these sessions.

Q3: The Holy Trinity

Catechism: 232–267, 683–690

Objectives

Participants will…

- describe the Trinity as an eternal communion of three divine persons: Father, Son, and Spirit.
- cite examples of the Trinity revealed in Scripture and in the life of the Church.
- reflect on their relationship with each person of the Trinity.

Leader Meditation

Matthew 3:13–17

Think about your relationship to the Blessed Trinity. When you pray, do you tend to pray to the Father, to the Son, or to the Holy Spirit? If there is one person you tend to overlook, pray now for a deeper relationship with this divine person.

Related *Catholic Updates*

- "The Trinity: Mystery at the Heart of Life" (C8807A)
- "Who Is the Holy Spirit?" (C9506A)

Leader Preparation

- Read the lesson handout, this lesson plan, the opening Scripture passage, and the *Catechism* sections. Be prepared to respond to common questions posed by inquirers with little to no concept of God, as well as from candidates whose perception of God focuses only on the person of Jesus.
- Be familiar with the vocabulary terms in this lesson: (Most Holy or Blessed) Trinity, mystery, Incarnation, (divine) person, doxology. Definitions can be found in this guide's glossary.
- Gather copies of the Nicene Creed for participants. If proclaimed aloud, consider reading from a missalette, worship aid, or liturgical book.
- Reflect on the shield of the Trinity. This and other visual aides can help the group conceptualize these mysteries. Many are familiar with St. Patrick's use of the cloverleaf or shamrock.
- Gather some prayers to the Trinity—both those directed at one particular divine person as well as others invoking or listing all three or God as a whole. Demonstrating both ancient and new, formal and casual, will add variety and deepen the group's sense of each person's identity.

Welcome

As the group gathers, welcome any new inquirers and sponsors. Check for supplies and immediate needs. Solicit questions or comments about the previous session and/or share new information and findings. Begin promptly.

Opening Scripture

Matthew 3:13–17

Light the candle, and then read the passage aloud from a Catholic Bible or study *Lectionary*. Allow for a moment of silence, and then invite comments or reactions to the words. Ask participants, "What's your image of God?"

> "The mystery of the Most Holy Trinity is the central mystery of Christian faith and life. It is the mystery of God in himself. It is therefore the source of all the other mysteries of faith, the light that enlightens them." *CCC 234*

Q3 INQUIRY

In Short:

- The Trinity is three persons in one God.
- The Trinity is revealed in Scripture.
- We can relate to each person of God.

The Holy Trinity

> *"The Father is God, the Son is God, and the Holy Spirit is God, and yet they are not three but one God."*
>
> *Athanasian Creed*

Catholics often begin prayers with the sign of the cross and the words: "In the name of the Father, and of the Son, and of the Holy Spirit." By doing so, we express our faith in three divine persons collectively called the Holy or Blessed **Trinity**. This simple yet meaningful prayer connects us to a mystery at the heart of Christian life and belief. In fact, "the Most Holy Trinity is the central mystery of Christian faith and life" (*CCC* 234).

The Church calls it a **mystery** because three persons in one God is difficult to comprehend. It's not a mystery in the sense some genius or advancement in science will someday solve it. It's a mystery in the religious sense, a deep truth or reality beyond anything we can experience or understand in this world. The heart of the mystery of the Holy Trinity is that "God himself is an eternal exchange of love, Father, Son, and Holy Spirit, and he has destined us to share in that exchange" (*CCC* 221).

This mystery is like "love" or "grace." As much as God reveals to us, as vivid as our experiences are, we know there's always something more.

We're called to loving communion with others because we are created in God's image. It's often through human relationships that we experience God's love.

- *What relationships have helped you experience God's love?*

The Trinity in the Bible

Belief in the Trinity has been part of the Christian understanding of God from the beginnings of the Church. Saint Paul wrote in the year 57: "The grace of the Lord Jesus Christ and the love of God and the fellowship of the Holy Spirit be with all of you" (2 Corinthians 13:13). That greeting recognizes three persons in God.

This mystery of God's life and identity was revealed in Scripture gradually:

1. The Father revealed himself to ancient Israel. In a world that worshiped many gods, he taught the Israelites that he is the one God who created the world. The Old Testament hints at the Trinity. God created the world by his "word" and "breath" (Psalm 33:6). The Word (Son) of God and his life-giving breath (Spirit) are active throughout the Old Testament.
2. Next came the Son, revealed in the Incarnation: "In the beginning was the

ADULTS

CCC 232–267, 683–690

The Holy Trinity

Point out how the participants' own images of God relate to the three persons of the Trinity present in this session's opening Scripture (Jesus' baptism). Remind them that the Trinity is one of the great mysteries of our faith.

Read or paraphrase the following from the *U.S. Catholic Catechism for Adults*: "We do not confuse the word *mystery* with the term as it applies to a detective story or a scientific puzzle. The mystery of God is not a puzzle to be solved. It is a truth to be reverenced. It is a reality too rich to be fully grasped by our minds, so that while it continues to unfold, it always remains mostly beyond our comprehension. The mystery of God is present in our lives and yet remains hidden, beyond the full grasp of our minds" (51).

Invite volunteers to read the text aloud, then pause to let these truths sink in.

The Trinity in the Bible

Review God's three-step revelation. As participants explore the Trinity in the Bible, focus on God as one, the Incarnation, and Pentecost.

Emphasize that the Trinity, while one, was revealed gradually—and yet, all three persons are present in Scripture and throughout salvation history.

Remind participants that God's presence in Scripture will be further covered in lesson *Q6 Divine Revelation*.

Speaking of God

Refer to the *Catechism* and Creed to explain some of the terms in the lesson that describe the relationship among the Father, Son, and Spirit. While they may seem vague or technical, they create a common language and answer the question: "How can there be three Gods in one?"

Explain that the text of the Creed is proclaimed by every Catholic during Mass. If your parish uses the Apostles' Creed, point this out but refer to the Nicene Creed during this session. Without going through the entire Creed, show participants how:

- The Creed begins with "I believe in one God."
- The first section is about God the Father.
- The second section is about Jesus the Son.
- The third section is about the Holy Spirit.

Pose these questions as a review:

- Father, Son and Spirit are one (God, divine being, substance, nature, essence, etc.).
- Father, Son, and Spirit are three (distinct yet wholly divine persons).
- Father, Son and Spirit are distinguished by their (relationship to/communion with one another).
- We believe in one (God/divine being) in three (persons) who live in eternal (relationship or communion) with each other.

Word, and the Word was with God, and the Word was God….And the Word became flesh and made his dwelling among us, and we saw his glory, the glory as of the Father's only Son" (John 1:1, 14). We celebrate the **Incarnation**: God's coming to dwell with us on earth as the Son (Jesus) in human flesh, at Christmas.

When used to refer to Jesus, "the title 'Son of God' signifies the *unique and eternal* relationship of Jesus Christ to God his Father" (*CCC* 454, emphasis added). This means that in the very life of God, there is a Father-Son relationship: God "is Father not only in being Creator; he is eternally Father in relation to his only Son" (*CCC* 240). The Father and Son are so close, they share one divine nature.

3. Finally, the Holy Spirit was sent and revealed. At Jesus' baptism, there is a manifestation of each person of the Trinity: the Son is baptized, the Father speaks, and the Spirit descends like a dove:

> ***"Jesus came from Galilee to John at the Jordan to be baptized by him….After Jesus was baptized, he came up from the water and behold, the heavens were opened [for him], and he saw the Spirit of God descending like a dove [and] coming upon him. And a voice came from the heavens, saying, 'This is my beloved Son, with whom I am well pleased.'"***
>
> *Matthew 3:13, 16–17*

As his death was approaching, Jesus began to speak of the promised Spirit he will send after his resurrection (John 14:16–17, 26). Jesus' words are fulfilled when the Spirit is poured out on the Church on the day of Pentecost, fifty days after his resurrection on Easter. On that day, the Spirit is "manifested, given, and communicated as a divine person….On that day, the Holy Trinity is fully revealed" (*CCC* 731–732). Sharing in the one divine nature, the Holy Spirit is both the Spirit of the Father and the Spirit of the Son (*CCC* 245).

In the history of salvation, the three persons of the Trinity are revealed in order: Father, Son, and Spirit. In our own spiritual histories, we also come to know each divine person but not always in that order. Some may come to know Jesus first and only later develop a relationship with the Father and the Spirit.

- *Which person of the Trinity feels most approachable to you right now? Why? Which person do you look forward to getting to know more about?*

Speaking of God: A Vocabulary of Faith

A good way to learn what Catholics believe is to look at the words of our prayers. The Nicene Creed, an important statement of our beliefs, spells out our belief in the three persons in one God:

- It begins by saying that we "believe in one God"—one being, one consciousness, one will, one mind, a single, infinite, all-powerful, divine reality. The Church uses terms such as "substance," "essence," and "nature" to describe this oneness (*CCC* 252–253). God's goodness and power is shared in three persons. Each **person** is complete and distinct from the others yet wholly and eternally God.

- "The Father almighty" is "maker of heaven and earth." We see the Father as the Creator and cause of everything.
- Jesus is "the Only Begotten Son of God, born of the Father before all ages." This means that the Son *always was.* Both Father and Son have existed from the beginning and have been in the closest of relationships: "The Father and I are one" (John 10:30).
- The Holy Spirit "proceeds from the Father and the Son." The Spirit issues from them both—together and eternally, *not after* in time or in order.

The words "begotten" and "proceeds" both convey energy, movement, and power, in the context of unity, equality, and love. Seeing a dynamic relationship among equals is key to understanding the Trinity.

An Image of the Trinity

Any attempt to visualize the Trinity is going to be limited and imperfect because God is more than we can fully understand. However, the shield of the Trinity, though imperfect, may help.

The points of the triangle represent *who* God is: the three persons. The Father is not the Son; the Son is not the Father; and the Spirit is neither the Father nor the Son (CCC 254).

Father, Son, and Spirit are one in what they are but distinct in who they are.

The Work of the Trinity

"Inseparable in what they are, the divine persons are also inseparable in what they do."

CCC 267

Each person of the Trinity works in common with the others in every divine action. All the saving work of God proceeds from the Father, through the Son, toward completion in the Spirit. The goal of the Trinity in creation and history is to unite human beings with the love of the triune God (*CCC* 260). We receive this call to share in a life of divine love "by the grace of Baptism 'in the name of the Father and of the Son and of the Holy Spirit'" (*CCC* 265). Saint Paul beautifully expresses this experience of grace:

"When the fullness of time had come, God sent his Son, born of a woman…to ransom [us]…so that we might receive adoption. As proof that you are children, God sent the Spirit of his Son into our hearts, crying out, 'Abba, Father!'"

Galatians 4:4–6

An Image of the Trinity

Refer to the image as you review the relationship among the three persons. Invite participants to share their reactions or any other metaphor for the Trinity as well as new thoughts and connections they are making.

Remind them that no metaphor or image is entirely accurate or reflective of God's fullness.

The Work of the Trinity

Clarify that the work of the Trinity is a single effort, the work of one God. Ask participants, "What might this work of God be?" Point out (read aloud) one good answer from the lesson: "The goal of the Trinity in creation and history is to unite human beings with the love of the triune God (*CCC* 260)."

Point out that the Trinitarian formula ("In the name of the Father and of the Son and of the Holy Spirit") is *required* for a valid baptism. Because Catholics believe in God as Trinity, baptism in the name of Jesus alone is insufficient.

Introduce participants to looking up Bible verses before you begin the activity. First model the steps to find one passage—book, chapter, verse—then allow participants time to practice.

Complete the activity as a group or in small teams as time allows. *Share these responses with the group as needed.*

- *God the Father*
Matthew 19:4 ("Creator"); Romans 8:15 ("*Abba*, Father"); 2 Corinthians 1:3 ("Father of our Lord Jesus Christ, the Father of compassion and God of all encouragement…")

- *God the Son*
Matthew 1:23 ("'Emmanuel,' which means 'God is with us.'"); John 1:14 ("the Word became flesh…the Father's only Son"); John 10:11 ("the good shepherd")

- *God the Spirit*
Matthew 3:16 ("a dove"); John 15:26 ("the Advocate…the Spirit of truth"); Acts 2:1–4 ("a strong driving wind…tongues as of fire")

Using the Bible passages below, find names, roles, or characteristics for each person of the Trinity.

God the Father

Matthew 19:4 ____________________

Romans 8:15 ____________________

2 Corinthians 1:3 ____________________

God the Son

Matthew 1:23 ____________________

John 1:14 ____________________

John 10:11 ____________________

God the Spirit

Matthew 3:16 ____________________

John 15:26 ____________________

Acts 2:1–4 ____________________

Praying to the Trinity

Through prayer to each divine person, we enter into an experience of the Trinity that overcomes our limited ability to grasp this mystery.

Saint Ignatius of Loyola offers an easy yet powerful method of prayer that can help us grow in our relationship with the Trinity. He encourages us to end each time of prayer or meditation with a conversation in which we speak to each divine person in short, spontaneous, heartfelt phrases, much like a friend speaking to a friend:

1. First, speak to the Father whatever is on your heart, expressing your gratitude, sharing your needs and worries.
2. Then speak to Jesus in the same way.
3. Finally, speak to the Spirit, asking for help and guidance.

In your journal, write three short prayers using the prompts below:

Dear Heavenly Father…

Dear Jesus, my Lord and Savior…

Come, Holy Spirit, help me…

Try to begin and end each day this week with a short prayer to the Father, Son, and Holy Spirit.

Journey of Faith for Adults: Inquiry, Q3 (826252)
Imprimi Potest: Stephen T. Rehrauer, CSsR, Provincial, Denver Province, the Redemptorists
Imprimatur: "In accordance with CIC 827, permission to publish has been granted on March 7, 2016, by the Most Reverend Edward M. Rice, Auxiliary Bishop, Archdiocese of St. Louis. Permission to publish is an indication that nothing contrary to Church teaching is contained in this work. It does not imply any endorsement of the opinions expressed in the publication; nor is any liability assumed by this permission."

Contributing writers: John L. Gresham, PhD, Leonard Foley, OFM, and Karen Berry, OSF. Editors of 2016 edition: Denise Bossert, Julia DiSalvo, and Joan McKamey. Design: Lorena Mitre Jimenez. Images: Shutterstock.

Liguori PUBLICATIONS
A Redemptorist Ministry
Printed in the United States of America. 20 19 18 17 16 / 5 4 3 2 1. Third Edition.

Praying to the Trinity

Explain that we can pray to God as one (using names such as God, Lord, Holy Trinity) and we can pray to each person of the Trinity.

Remind participants that they may be more comfortable praying to one person of the Trinity at any given time and that their relationships with the divine persons will grow. The important thing is that they pray to our one, true God.

Display or distribute, then recite, a few prayers to the Trinity or to a divine person. Reference the prayers discussed earlier.

Journaling

Read the three prompts from the lesson aloud. Ask participants to spend this week addressing prayers in their journals to each person of the Trinity.

Closing Prayer

End with a sign of the cross and recitation of the Glory Be or the following prayer:

"O Sanctissima"

O most Holy Trinity, I adore you who dwell by your grace in my soul. Sanctify me more and more, make me love you more and more, abide with me evermore and be my true joy. Amen.

Take-home

Remind participants to pray to each person of the Trinity this week. Suggest they give extra attention to the person they most overlook as they reflect on the mysteries of God.

Q4: Who Is Jesus Christ?

Catechism: 422–682

Objectives

Participants will…

- identify Jesus as fully human and fully divine: as a real, historical being and as the one, true God.
- describe Christ as the way to the Father and salvation, as the truth, and as the fullness and source of life.
- begin or nurture a personal relationship with Jesus.

Leader Meditation

John 10:7–18

Jesus likens himself to a shepherd who lays down his life for his sheep. What do these words tell you about the person of Jesus? Ask Jesus in prayer to be your shepherd and guide as you lead this lesson.

Related *Catholic Updates*

- "Finding the Heart of Jesus' Life: Looking at Jesus in the Gospels" (C0312A)
- "Four Faces of Jesus" (C1305A)
- "Who Is Jesus?" (C8509A)

Leader Preparation

- Read the lesson handout, this lesson plan, the opening Scripture passage, and the *Catechism* sections.
- Be familiar with the vocabulary terms in this lesson: *ichthys*, Messiah, miracle. Definitions can be found in the lesson and in this guide's glossary.
- Be prepared to review how to look up Bible verses. This lesson has many, so determine ahead of time whether you can cover them all, divide them up, or have participants reflect on some outside of the session.
- Ask your pastor for guidance on relating Jesus' life, identity, words, and dual natures to participants. Perhaps he can help to lead the session or recommend some additional material on these subjects.

Welcome

Welcome the participants and sponsors, especially any new attendees. Check for supplies and immediate needs. Solicit questions about the previous session and/or share new information. Begin promptly.

Opening Scripture

John 10:7–18

Light the candle and read the passage aloud. Ask, "What does this passage tell us about Jesus?" Discuss the meaning of Jesus' words: "I am the good shepherd, and I know mine and mine know me…" (10:14). Ask, "Who does Jesus call his 'own?'"

> "Taken up to heaven and glorified after he had thus fully accomplished his mission, Christ dwells on earth in his Church."
>
> *CCC 669*

Q4 INQUIRY

In Short:

- Christ is the way to the Father and salvation.
- Jesus is fully human and fully divine.
- You can have a personal relationship with Jesus.

"Moved by the grace of the Holy Spirit and drawn by the Father, we believe in Jesus and confess: 'You are the Christ, the Son of the living God.'"

CCC 424

"To confess that Jesus is Lord is distinctive of Christian faith."

CCC 202

Who Is Jesus Christ?

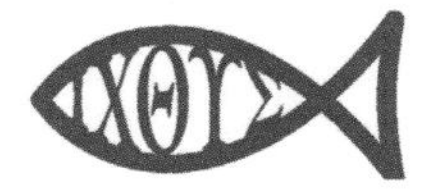

What do you see in the image at right? Early Christians used the fish symbol as a secret code indicating they were followers of Jesus. Sometimes the fish's eye was a tiny cross. You also see the Greek acronym ***ichthys***. Each letter (*iota, chi, theta, upsilon, sigma*) begins the words in the title "Jesus Christ, Son of God, Savior." When early Christians saw the fish or ichthys, they knew immediately they had met another Christian and were safe from persecution. They belonged to each other and to the Lord.

While the Catholic faith uses many symbols to illustrate deeper truths, our faith is founded in the living person of Jesus Christ. Jesus binds us to God and to each other. Christ alone gives meaning to our faith, and every belief and practice points to him, interrelating with the others to make up a complete and full expression of the truth.

Jesus' True Identity

Jesus' earthly existence is undeniable; historical research has established the approximate date and place of his birth, as well as the circumstances surrounding his crucifixion. Those around him felt certain of his origins, calling him "the carpenter, the son of Mary" and "the Nazarene" (Mark 6:3; 14:67; see also Matthew 13:55).

The real question, then, lies in whether Jesus is God—whether his miracles, teachings, death, and resurrection have real and lasting meaning for all humanity. Even in his own time and region, many were skeptical. The Jews were awaiting the Messiah, but they expected a mighty warrior. They never imagined their savior would have such humble beginnings. When Jesus asked his apostles, "Who do people say that I am?" (Mark 8:27), answers varied. Peter replied, "the Messiah." Jesus didn't deny this identification but "warned them not to tell anyone" (8:29–30).

ADULTS

CCC 422–682

Who Is Jesus Christ?

Invite the sponsors or candidates to share a personal experience in which God revealed himself as Lord and/or Savior. This could be a moment of conversion, acceptance, profession of faith, or salvific mercy. Their responses serve as a personal answer to the lesson's question, "How has he guided your life so far?"

Jesus' True Identity

Compare who Jesus was to his contemporaries and who he is to us today. Invite participants to share how they view and feel about Christ now, and what they hope their relationship with him will be like. Encourage them to let Jesus lead the way rather than attempt to force a concept of Jesus into their existing mindset.

Discuss why Jesus didn't deny Peter's identification but "warned them not to tell anyone" (8:29–30).

Jesus himself tells us, "The works that the Father gave me to accomplish, these works that I perform testify on my behalf that the Father has sent me" (John 5:36).

Discuss how learning a truth that conflicts with what you believe can be hard to accept or how we determine whether or not something is true. Emphasize that we know Jesus is the truth and that Jesus as truth is the center of our faith.

Complete the Bible activities together. Depending on your group's size and time, you may assign items to pairs or tables or simply read a few aloud.

Share these responses to "How did Jesus describe himself?" as needed:

- John 4:25–26 ("the Messiah…the Anointed") the promised leader and savior of the Israelites
- John 6:48 ("the bread of life") a source of spiritual nourishment and divine communion
- John 8:12 ("the light of the world") a source of revelation and truth
- John 10:14–15 ("the good shepherd") a faithful protector and guide
- John 11:25–27 ("the resurrection and the life…the Messiah, the Son of God")
- John 15:1 ("the true vine") our connection and bond to God
- John 17:1–3 ("your son…the one whom you sent") God's divine agent

---

Messiah: In Hebrew, "anointed" (Greek, *christos*). The one foretold by prophets who would deliver God's people from their enemies, sin, and evil and establish a kingdom of justice and salvation. Similar to *savior*, this term originally had a clear political sense but later was revealed to have deeper, more supernatural implications.

> *"Know for certain that God has made him both Lord and Messiah, this Jesus whom you crucified."*
>
> *Acts 2:36*

- *If Jesus is God and Savior, what does that mean for your life?*

Only Jesus can reveal the secret of his person. If we are to understand him, we must let Jesus speak for himself.

How did Jesus describe himself?

John 4:25–26	John 6:48
John 8:12	John 10:14–15
John 11:25–27	John 15:1
John 17:1–3	

- *Which of the verses from John's Gospel has the most meaning for you? Why?*

Jesus Is the Way

> *"I am the way and the truth and the life."*
>
> *John 14:6*

Jesus' identity and role can be difficult to understand and accept, yet over thousands of years, billions of people around the globe have called themselves followers of Christ. Many have changed or lost their lives because of it.

It's important to realize that Jesus was a faithful Jew. The Jews possessed a deep knowledge of God. Drawing on this background, Jesus shared many sayings that were taught by the prophets and Jewish rabbis. For example, Jesus taught that we should pray in secret (Matthew 6:6). A Jewish saying shares a similar message: "He who prays within his house surrounds it with a wall that is stronger than iron."

What made Jesus unique, then, isn't his teaching. Jesus is unique because *he is the Son of God*. He not only called people to hear and heed his message, but also to believe in him! That was completely new; prophets and teachers had never before demanded belief in themselves. They wanted to kill him, we're told, because he "called God his own Father, making himself equal to God" (John 5:18).

Jesus placed himself above the Jewish religious leaders and practices. He claimed to be the way to God and the complete fulfillment of Jewish teachings and prophecies. He said, "Do not think that I have come to abolish the law or the prophets. I have come not to abolish but to fulfill" (Matthew 5:17; see also Luke 24:44).

- *To what or where do Jesus' life and teachings lead you?*
- *How has he guided your life so far?*

Jesus Is the Truth

> *"For this I was born and for this I came into the world, to testify to the truth."*
>
> John 18:37

Jesus says, "I am the truth," not "I speak the truth" or "I reveal the truth," but "I am the truth." As son of Mary and Son of God, Jesus' human and divine natures cannot be separated. Unlike religious leaders and saints throughout history, he is never "off duty" or subject to sin and flaws. Every word, every action, every gesture, every emotion is full of meaning and truth. Jesus invites us to have a personal relationship with him—and in him and through him, a relationship with the Father.

> *"To fall in love with God is the greatest romance; to seek him the greatest adventure; to find him, the greatest human achievement."*
>
> St. Augustine

Jesus came to show us God in human terms—to make the Father present to all.

How does Jesus describe his relationship with the Father in John's Gospel?

John 1:18	John 5:37–38
John 6:46	John 8:38

- *What would it mean for you to have a personal relationship with Jesus? Does this seem more appealing or uncomfortable? Why?* ?

Jesus Is the Life

The greatest treasure we have is life itself. Our earthly life is fragile, limited, and temporary, but Christ offers us a full and everlasting life. For many, it takes a close encounter with our own limits or mortality to seek the life Christ offers and true salvation.

How does Jesus show himself to be the life in the following Scripture passages:

Matthew 16:25	Mark 8:35
John 1:3–4	John 5:21, 24
John 6:53	John 10:10
John 17:1–2	

This life includes being filled with the Holy Spirit, "the Lord, the giver of life" (Nicene Creed). Jesus promised to send the Spirit. When he came upon the apostles at Pentecost, fifty days after Jesus' resurrection at Easter, they were filled with new life—the life of the risen Christ.

> *"I live, no longer I, but Christ lives in me."*
>
> Galatians 2:20

Jesus continues to promise his life and Spirit to anyone who wishes to be united to him. Having a personal relationship with Christ, which includes prayer and the sacraments, is how disciples embrace the Trinity and prepare for life after death.

Jesus Is the Truth

Clarify the Catholic teaching of Jesus' dual nature: Christ is *fully* human *and fully* divine. His being or essence is not "half and half"; his divine nature was not diminished by the Incarnation, nor was his humanity reduced by being without sin. This should give us hope in his ability as a redeemer and in our ability to become holy.

Explain that throughout the Gospels, Jesus doesn't claim only to lead others to the Father but to *be one* with the Father, that is, to be God in the flesh.

Share these responses to "How does he describe his relationship with the Father...?" as needed:

- John 1:18
("No one has ever seen God. The only Son...has revealed him.") Jesus is the image of the Father, the full revelation of God.

- John 5:37–38
("You have never heard his voice nor seen his form...because you do not believe in the one whom he has sent.") Jesus claims justification by the Father. He is the voice and Word of God.

- John 6:46
("Not that anyone has seen the Father except the one who is from God.") Jesus possesses full knowledge of the Father.

- John 8:38
("I tell you what I have seen in the Father's presence; then do what you have heard from the Father.") Jesus manifests the Father. He transmits God's knowledge and truth to the disciples (Church).

Jesus Is the Life

Emphasize why we should come to know Jesus: so that we may know God (John 14:8–9) and receive freedom from sin and eternal life (John 8:31–32).

Explain that salvation and life with God in heaven comes from faith in Christ alone.

Share these responses to "How does Jesus show himself to be the life" as needed:

- Matthew 16:25; Mark 8:35
("Whoever loses his life for my sake will find it.") By giving our lives to Christ, we receive eternal life.

- John 1:3–4
("What came to be through him was life...") Christ's life frees us from sin and doubt and is a "light" to the truth.

- John 5:21, 24
("Just as the Father raises the dead and gives life, so also does the Son give life...") Faith in Christ and knowledge of God's word saves us from sin and death.

- John 6:53
("Unless you eat the flesh of the Son of Man and drink his blood, you do not have life within you.") Christ's life is present and received in the Eucharist.

• John 10:10
("I came so that they might have life…") Jesus was sent to save all humanity.

• John 17:1–2
("Give glory to your son…so that he may give eternal life to all you gave him.") The Son has authority to grant us life.

The Miracles of Jesus

Distinguish the lesson's definition of *miracle* from our everyday use of the term. Invite the group to compare examples of events we commonly refer to as "miracles" with Church-approved miracles (used to declare sainthood). Ask, "How might our everyday definition of *miracle* fall short? How does the Church's definition witness to the reality of God?"

Discuss as many of the miracles as possible.

Suggested responses are below:

• *Wedding at Cana*
(John 2:1–11) Sign of his divinity and affirmation of Mary's faith in him.

• *Cleansing of a leper*
(Matthew 8:1–4) Affirmation of the leper's faith.

• *Healing the centurion's servant*
(Luke 7:1–10) Affirmation of the centurion's faith (see 7:9).

• *Healing Jairus' daughter and the woman with a hemorrhage*

(Matthew 9:18–26; Mark 5:21–43; Luke 8:40–56) Affirmation(s).

• *Loaves and Fishes/Feeding 5,000*
(Matthew 14:13–21; Mark 6:34–44; Luke 9:10–17; John 6:1–15) Sign of his divinity and mission to feed us with spiritual/divine "bread."

• *Walking on water*
(Mark 6:45–52) Sign of his divinity and to strengthen the disciples' faith.

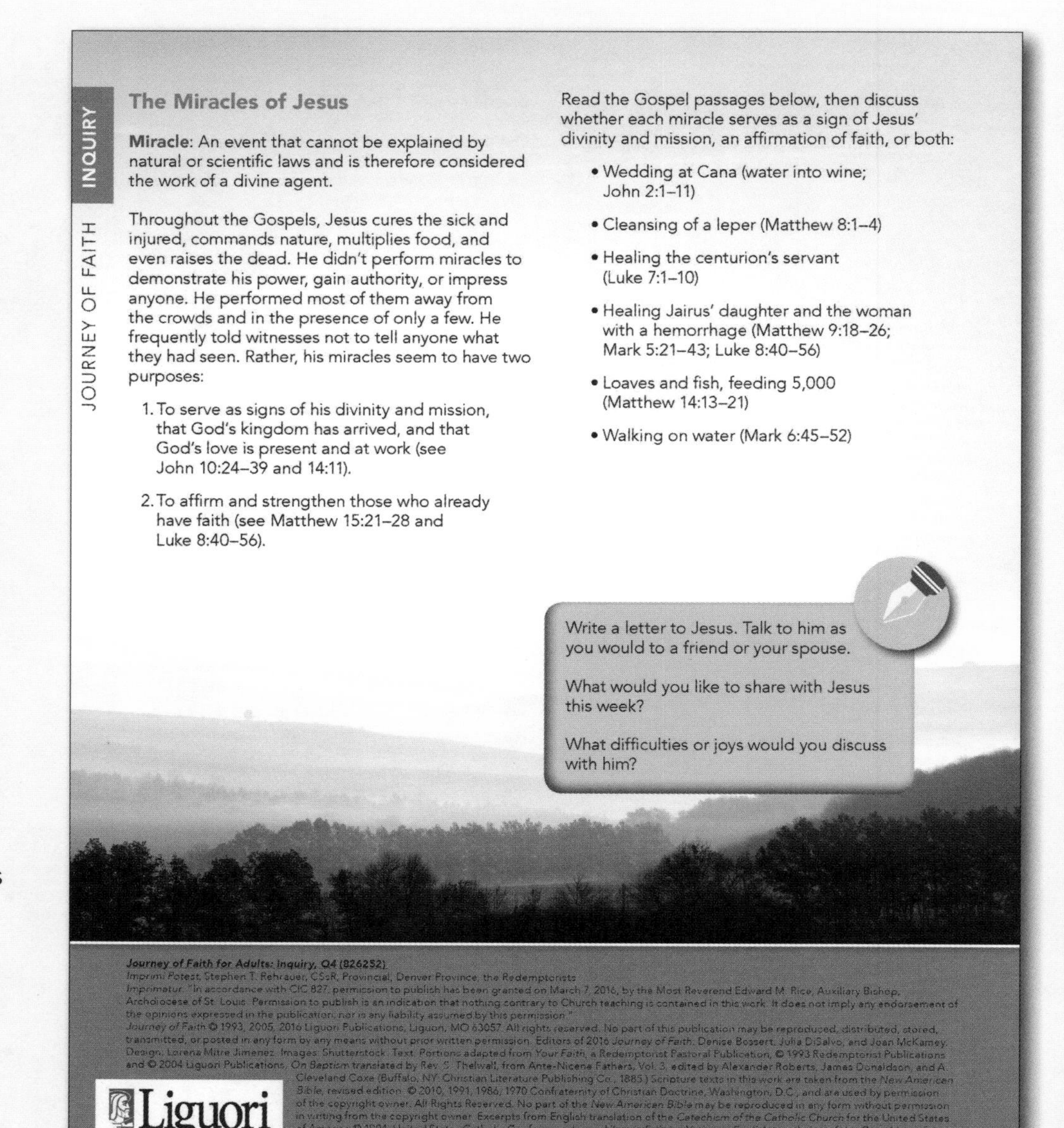

INQUIRY

JOURNEY OF FAITH

The Miracles of Jesus

Miracle: An event that cannot be explained by natural or scientific laws and is therefore considered the work of a divine agent.

Throughout the Gospels, Jesus cures the sick and injured, commands nature, multiplies food, and even raises the dead. He didn't perform miracles to demonstrate his power, gain authority, or impress anyone. He performed most of them away from the crowds and in the presence of only a few. He frequently told witnesses not to tell anyone what they had seen. Rather, his miracles seem to have two purposes:

1. To serve as signs of his divinity and mission, that God's kingdom has arrived, and that God's love is present and at work (see John 10:24–39 and 14:11).
2. To affirm and strengthen those who already have faith (see Matthew 15:21–28 and Luke 8:40–56).

Read the Gospel passages below, then discuss whether each miracle serves as a sign of Jesus' divinity and mission, an affirmation of faith, or both:

- Wedding at Cana (water into wine; John 2:1–11)
- Cleansing of a leper (Matthew 8:1–4)
- Healing the centurion's servant (Luke 7:1–10)
- Healing Jairus' daughter and the woman with a hemorrhage (Matthew 9:18–26; Mark 5:21–43; Luke 8:40–56)
- Loaves and fish, feeding 5,000 (Matthew 14:13–21)
- Walking on water (Mark 6:45–52)

Write a letter to Jesus. Talk to him as you would to a friend or your spouse.

What would you like to share with Jesus this week?

What difficulties or joys would you discuss with him?

Journey of Faith for Adults: Inquiry, Q4 (826252)
Imprimi Potest: Stephen T. Rehrauer, CSsR, Provincial, Denver Province, the Redemptorists
Imprimatur: "In accordance with CIC 827, permission to publish has been granted on March 7, 2016, by the Most Reverend Edward M. Rice, Auxiliary Bishop, Archdiocese of St. Louis. Permission to publish is an indication that nothing contrary to Church teaching is contained in this work. It does not imply any endorsement of the opinions expressed in the publication; nor is any liability assumed by this permission."

Editors of 2016 *Journey of Faith*: Denise Bossert, Julia DiSalvo, and Joan McKamey. Design: Lorena Mitre Jimenez. Images: Shutterstock. Text: Portions adapted from *Your Faith*, a Redemptorist Pastoral Publication, © 1993 Redemptorist Publications and © 2004 Liguori Publications. *On Baptism* translated by Rev. S. Thelwall, from Ante-Nicene Fathers, Vol. 3, edited by Alexander Roberts, James Donaldson, and A. Cleveland Coxe (Buffalo, NY: Christian Literature Publishing Co., 1885.) Scripture texts in this work are taken from the *New American Bible*, revised edition © 2010, 1991, 1986, 1970 Confraternity of Christian Doctrine, Washington, D.C., and are used by permission of the copyright owner. All Rights Reserved. No part of the *New American Bible* may be reproduced in any form without permission in writing from the copyright owner. Excerpts from English translation of the *Catechism of the Catholic Church* for the United States of America © 1994, United States Catholic Conference, Inc. —*Libreria Editrice Vaticana*. English translation of the *Catechism of the Catholic Church: Modifications from the Editio Typica* © 1997, United States Catholic Conference, Inc. —*Libreria Editrice Vaticana*. Compliant with *The Roman Missal, Third Edition*.
Printed in the United States of America. 20 19 18 17 16 / 5 4 3 2 1. Third Edition.

Liguori PUBLICATIONS
A Redemptorist Ministry

Journaling

Remind participants to complete this outside of the session.

Closing Prayer

Teach and pray aloud one of the memorial acclamations below. Explain that these statements summarize our faith and declare who Jesus is. They are so important, they are sung or recited (proclaimed) by the entire assembly at every Mass.

1. *We proclaim your Death, O Lord, and profess your Resurrection until you come again.*
2. *When we eat this Bread and drink this Cup, we proclaim your Death, O Lord, until you come again.*
3. *Save us, Savior of the world, for by your Cross and Resurrection you have set us free.*

Take-home

Encourage participants to continue observing Jesus in Scripture and to deeply contemplate who Jesus is in their lives. The more they hear the voice of God, the clearer it will become, and the closer he will seem. Invite them to complete any unfinished activities and the journaling and to reread any verses that spoke to them. John 1:1–18 will help them reflect on what it means for Jesus to be God's Word incarnate.

Q5: The Bible

Catechism: 74–83, 101–133, 109–119

Objectives

Participants will…

- recall the historicity, structure, and nature of the Bible.
- describe Scripture as the sacred and inspired word of God.
- consider context when reading and interpreting Scripture.

Leader Meditation

2 Timothy 3:16–17

Consider whether you take sufficient time each week to read and reflect on Scripture. Ask yourself, "When and how has God guided me through this text and helped me make decisions about my life?" Then pray the prayer below:

Dear God, you have given me the task of helping inquirers understand your Word. At times I still struggle to understand it fully myself. Please send down your Spirit to inspire and speak through me, that I may become a bridge that connects your heart to the hearts and minds of my participants. Amen.

Related *Catholic Updates*

- "The Whole Bible at a Glance: Its 'Golden Thread' of Meaning" (C8904A)
- "Celebrating God's Word: How Catholics Read the Bible" (C1406A)

Leader Preparation

- Read the lesson, this lesson plan, the Scripture passage, and the *Catechism* sections.
- Be familiar with the terms: Bible, salvation history, (divinely) inspired, Torah, Gospel, epistle, testament, covenant, canon, Scriptures, inerrant. Definitions can be found in this guide's glossary.
- Make sure each participant has access to a Catholic Bible. Gather materials and resources that assist them in studying and reflecting on Scripture and the Mass readings.

Welcome

Greet each person as he or she arrives. Check for supplies and immediate needs. Solicit questions about the previous session and/or share new information and findings. Begin promptly.

Opening Scripture

2 Timothy 3:16–17

Light the candle and read the passage aloud. Ask, "What words, texts, or writings have helped you grow in faith, understand the truth, or become a better person?" Allow participants a moment to consider their answer, and then invite them to comment or react.

> "Sacred Scripture is the speech of God as it is put down in writing under the breath of the Holy Spirit….[It] must be read and interpreted in the light of the same Spirit by whom it was written."
>
> *Dei Verbum*, 9, 12; see *CCC* 81, 111

Q5 INQUIRY

In Short:

- The Bible has a unique nature, history, and structure.
- Scripture is the sacred and inspired word of God.
- Catholics consider context when reading and interpreting Scripture.

The Bible

In his book, *In God's Underground*, Richard Wurmbrand tells of his imprisonment in Romania for his religious views. One day, the guards brought in a new prisoner named Avram. Avram was badly injured and in an upper-body cast. After the guards left, his hand disappeared beneath the cast and emerged with a small, tattered book:

> *"Avram lay there quietly turning the pages, until he became conscious of the eager eyes fixed on him. 'Your book,' I said. 'What is it? Where did you get it?' Avram closed the book. 'It's the Gospel according to John,' he said." He had managed to conceal it under his cast at the time of his arrest. Avram held out the book. Wurmbrand says, "I took the little book in my hands as if it were a live bird. No life-saving drug could have been more precious to me...."*

- *What might you have risked smuggling in if you were in Avram's situation? Why?*
- *Why might the Gospel of John been so precious to Avram and Wurmbrand?*

What Is the Bible?

The **Bible** ("little books" in Greek) is a collection of writings—a library—about God, his relationship with humankind, and how he wants us to relate to him and each other. As a whole, it serves as a record of **salvation history**: the Father's saving plan and works as recounted through time, people, and events, beginning with Adam and Eve in the Book of Genesis and ending in the new heaven and earth and fulfillment of God's kingdom in the Book of Revelation.

Who Wrote the Bible?

Many Bible stories and records were passed by word of mouth through oral tradition long before anyone wrote them down. These stories, also called Scriptures, were all written for different reasons but have the common purpose to try to share the story of God's relationship with his people. Eventually, people recognized a need to write them down. The books of the Bible were written at various times between 900 BC and AD 100.

CCC 422–682

ADULTS

Q5

The Bible

Discuss how participants approached (or didn't) the Bible before coming to the RCIA. This will help you get a baseline for how familiar participants are with the Bible or how their former perspective may be at odds with Catholic teaching (such as taking the Bible as historical and scientific fact in all cases).

Ask if anyone has a favorite Bible verse or story. Invite the participant to read or relate it to the group, explaining why it is meaningful to him or her.

Who Wrote the Bible?

Participants may ask questions about the reliability of Scriptures. There is evidence both within Scriptures themselves and outside of it that roots them to historical events and eyewitness accounts. Encourage curious participants to continue exploring Catholic resources on the history of the Bible (*CCC Article 3: Sacred Scripture* is a good place to start.)

While the Bible should not be discussed as fiction, you should also explain the difficulties of using the Bible as a science text.

For example: Genesis teaches important truths about our faith and creation, but it wasn't written to give us a scientific explanation of creation. That was never its purpose. One way to think about it is that while Genesis doesn't tell us in scientific language how the world was created, it does explain why the world was created and who created it.

How Is the Old Testament Organized?

Review the Bible's organization and give examples from each section (for example, for prophetic books: Isaiah; for Pauline epistles: Ephesians).

Walk participants through how to look up today's reading from finding the correct book, to identifying where chapter and verse numbers occur within the text.

Emphasize that what unites the books of the Bible is not linear chronology, scientific analysis, or the preference of Church leaders, but the inspiration of the Spirit. The next lesson (*Q6 Divine Revelation*) will discuss this further.

Remind participants that there are 46 books of the Old Testament in Catholic versions of the Bible.

How is the New Testament Organized?

Remind participants that there are 27 books of the New Testament in Catholic versions of the Bible.

The authors came from different backgrounds and wrote in a variety of languages and styles. Catholics believe and teach that each book was divinely inspired. This means we believe the Holy Spirit guided the authors' work to ensure they expressed the message, the truth, that God wanted shared. Saying that God is the author of the Bible doesn't mean God dictated the Bible word for word.

How Is the Old Testament Organized?

The Old Testament books trace the relationship between the Israelites and the one God and Creator who acts in human history, guiding it with plan and purpose.

The Pentateuch ("five books" in Greek) is the first five books of the Bible and also is known as the **Torah** ("Law" in Hebrew, specifically the Law of Moses). It tells of the Israelites' journey as God's Chosen People through Abraham's path to Canaan and the exodus from slavery in Egypt.

The Historical Books cover the period from the Israelites' entry into the Promised Land around 1225 BC to the end of the Maccabean wars around 135 BC. Their view of world events sees God's guiding hand in everything.

The Wisdom Books are an artistic yet instructional search into the meaning of life. The authors use poetry, proverbs, sayings, and songs to face problems and questions of our origin and destiny, suffering, good and evil, right and wrong.

The Prophetic Books are the words of those who speak for God about important situations concerning God's Chosen People. Central to the prophets are themes of repentance and expectation of the Messiah.

How Is the New Testament Organized?

For years after his resurrection, missionaries spread the news about Jesus by word of mouth. Eventually, Christians decided to preserve their heritage in writing.

Most of the New Testament books were written by the end of the first century. The writings don't tell who Jesus was but who he is. Each book reveals a unique aspect of Jesus, guides the Church and Christian living, and has the power to change lives today.

The Gospels—Gospel means "good news." The four Gospels were written for different communities, but all record the words and deeds of Jesus, tell the story of his passion and death, and explain what they mean in light of his resurrection.

- The Gospel of Matthew focuses on Jesus' teachings.
- The Gospel of Mark tells about the public ministry and humanity of Jesus.
- The Gospel of Luke reveals Jesus' concern for the poor and women.
- The Gospel of John leads us into the mystery of Christ.

The Acts of the Apostles is an account of how the early Church lived and grew.

The Pauline Epistles consist of thirteen letters from St. Paul to local churches and the Letter to the Hebrews.

The Catholic Letters are seven letters by other apostles to the universal Church.

The Book of Revelation is a message of hope for persecuted Christians, promising Christ's ultimate triumph—not a prediction of the future.

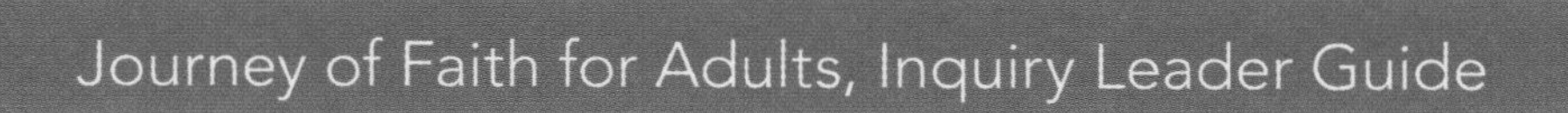

Two Testaments, Two Covenants

The word **testament** means "agreement" or "covenant." The concept of **covenant** is central to the Bible. The Old Covenant was established between God and our Jewish ancestors, beginning with Abraham. The New Covenant was established by and in Jesus Christ. The New Covenant fulfills and is a continuation of the Old. It extends God's law and salvation to Gentiles (non-Jews).

You have practiced looking up Bible verses in earlier lessons. Your Bible's table of contents will help you determine each book's respective testament and, likely, page number. The Old Testament comes first because its events occurred earlier. It is three times the size of the New Testament because it covers more books and more time. While the New Testament covers less than 100 years, it is far more important to Christians than the Old Testament.

Locate the passages below. First find the book, then the chapter, and finally the verses. What are some features and promises of the two covenants?

Exodus 19:3–8	Jeremiah 31:31–34
Luke 22:19–20	Hebrews 8:7–12

Where Did the Bible Come From?

By the middle of the first century AD, Christians had adopted the forty-six Old Testament books in the Greek translation. In the sixteenth century, Protestants adopted only the thirty-nine books in the Hebrew translation. In the year 393, bishops drew up the list of books in the New Testament. It included twenty-seven books that were widely used and accepted as inspired throughout the first centuries of Christianity. To be considered inspired, a book's content also had to be consistent with the message of Jesus as passed on by eyewitnesses.

Faced with alternate versions emerging out of the Protestant Reformation, the Council of Trent (1545–63) declared the list to be the **canon** (authentic and established collection) of sacred **Scripture** (in Latin, "writings"). This official declaration assured the faithful that the Catholic Scriptures were, indeed, sacred.

INQUIRY | JOURNEY OF FAITH

- *The canon of Scripture is a major part of the Church's legacy. What possessions or traditions are part of your family's heritage?*

How Do Catholics Read and Interpret Scripture?

The Bible's main purpose and intent is to impart the story of our relationship with God, not to detail historical events (although we do read about events in salvation history).

When we focus only on the words themselves (literal or surface reading), we can lose the deeper meaning behind those words. As you read passages from your Bible, ask yourself:

- What is the meaning and context of this passage?
- In what style or genre was it written?
- What historical or cultural influences are reflected here?
- What was the author's purpose or intent, given that he or she was inspired by the Holy Spirit?

Two Testaments, Two Covenants

Demonstrate how to find verses in the Bible by looking up one or two passages, if needed.

Review the four passages as a group so participants understand how the New Covenant relates to the Old Covenant and Christ's paschal mystery. Explain that not only is the Eucharist the fulfillment of the Jewish seder (Passover meal), but Christ's life and actions fulfilled the Old Testament prophecies.

Where Did the Bible Come From?

Respond to comments and questions about the reliability of Scriptures as needed. Participants may believe that Scripture is fiction or fictionalized by biased writers (or Church leaders) or through the "telephone" effect of relating accounts across centuries, nations, and cultures. However, there is evidence within and outside of Scripture that the books were written by, or closely connected to, *eyewitnesses* to the events, and that the books were written for the reader's and community's benefit (see earlier discussion of *divine inspiration*). Encourage participants to further study the history of the Bible, directing them to strong Catholic scholarly or apologetic material.

Share the story of the Dead Sea Scrolls if participants would benefit from additional historical evidence. The archaeological discovery of these Old Testament manuscripts supports Scripture's reliability and illustrate the continuity of Church teaching. Details and images can be found online at the Leon Levy Dead Sea Scrolls Digital Library and at the Israel Museum's Digital Dead Sea Scrolls site.

How Do Catholics Read and Interpret Scripture?

Remind participants that the Bible's main purpose and intent is to impart the story of our relationship with God, not to detail historical events, though events in salvation history are recounted.

If there's time or participants are struggling with this point, ask, "Are all Bible passages literal events or hard-and-fast rules, or do some simply illustrate guiding principles for our lives?" Explain that various passages may be one or all of these possibilities.

Emphasize the importance of understanding the book's literary form and the author's background and point of view. This means placing the passage into *its own* historical and cultural context. Point out that first-century biographies were not written in the same way as they are today.

Share the following passages, which illustrate the difference between fact and truth, as needed:

- Genesis 1
(The story of creation)

- Proverbs 24:3–5
("By wisdom a house is built…")

- Matthew 23:9
("Call no one on earth your father.")

• Luke 10:29–37
(The Good Samaritan – "Who is my neighbor?")

• Luke 15:11–32
(The Prodigal Son – "Your brother was dead and has come to life again.")

Shouldn't We Take the Bible Literally?

The Catholic Church believes that readers of the Bible must keep the meaning or purpose of a particular passage in mind rather than accepting every passage as literal fact. The Church, with the help of Scripture scholars, makes a distinction between truth and fact. While the Bible is inerrant (without mistakes) with regard to the truths it teaches because it has been divinely inspired, everything in the Bible is not fact.

Here is an example of a story often questioned.

Genesis is not meant to be read as a scientific description of creation. It was a profession of faith in the goodness of God and his creation. These are the truths we learn from the first several chapters of Genesis:

• God created the world.

• Everything God created was good.

• Man and woman were created in the image and likeness of God.

• Man and woman are the caretakers, or stewards, of God's magnificent creation.

• God's love for man and woman is perfect.

INQUIRY

JOURNEY OF FAITH

Shouldn't We Take the Bible Literally?

Some Bible passages are to be read literally. When we read that Jesus is the Messiah, those words should be taken literally. When Jesus says to eat his body and drink his blood, he is not speaking metaphorically (John 6:53–57). When we read about Jesus' death, resurrection, and ascension, we realize these were real events.

This doesn't mean every passage contains literal facts—only that each portion of the Bible conveys something real and important—a truth—about God or the Church. The Dogmatic Constitution on Divine Revelation (*Dei Verbum*), a document from the Second Vatican Council (1962–65), states that "the books of scripture, firmly, faithfully and without error, teach the truth which God, for the sake of our salvation, wished to see confided to the sacred scriptures" (11). In other words, the Bible is **inerrant**—incapable of being wrong—especially when it comes to salvation, faith, and morals. The Bible isn't to be read as a science or history book. It's a religious book with religious meaning.

Catholic teaching evolves and expands to address new situations and guides us in our interpretations and reflections on biblical texts. This makes it possible to accept scientific theories and historical conclusions without fear of contradicting God's word. When we read the Bible or hear it proclaimed at Mass, we can receive the message as God's will for our lives and communication from the one who loves each of us.

Choose and read a passage from the Bible, perhaps the Gospel for the coming Sunday.

What message of comfort, hope, or challenge do you find there?

Journey of Faith for Adults: Inquiry, Q5 (826252)
Imprimi Potest: Stephen T. Rehrauer, CSsR, Provincial, Denver Province, the Redemptorists
Imprimatur: "In accordance with CIC 827, permission to publish has been granted on March 7, 2016, by the Most Reverend Edward M. Rice, Auxiliary Bishop, Archdiocese of St. Louis. Permission to publish is an indication that nothing contrary to Church teaching is contained in this work. It does not imply any endorsement of the opinions expressed in the publication, nor is any liability assumed by this permission."

Printed in the United States of America. 20 19 18 17 16 / 5 4 3 2 1. Third Edition

Journaling

Reference or read the upcoming Sunday Mass readings, if there's time.

Closing Prayer

Read Hebrews 4:12 aloud, then tell participants that God speaks to them personally through Scripture. The books are not only for knowledge and reference but also for prayer. Conclude with this prayer:

O God, may your words remain with me, in my mind, on my lips, and in my heart. Dancing before my sorrow or joy, may their message of love not depart. For every joy has been written, and every sorrow has been consoled by your holy word, forever preserved, as each chapter and verse unfold. Amen.

Looking Ahead

Have participants capture their thoughts about how they and the Church, separately, view and use Scripture in their journal. Lesson *Q6 Divine Revelation* asks participants what Bible verses or passages have had special meaning in their lives. Encourage them to explore this question and to mark up their personal Bibles as they read and study it. Consider sharing information on parish or local Catholic Bible studies with those who are interested and ready.

Q6: Divine Revelation

Catechism: 27–100

Objectives

Participants will…

- describe revelation as God's gradual manifestation of himself and his saving works.
- recognize that God desires and grants us the means to know, love, and encounter him.
- cite multiple examples of ways we come to know God (see "Discussion," below).

Leader Meditation

John 16:13–15

Pray for growth and openness to God's revelations and plan for your life. Then ask, "Do I completely trust myself to God's divine plan?"

Related *Catholic Update*

"Scripture and Tradition: Revealing God's Plan" (C1306A)

Leader Preparation

- This lesson continues the discussion on faith and reason (science) that began in lesson Q2. Review that material along with this new material if needed.
- Be familiar with the terms: divine revelation, apostolic tradition, (sacred) Tradition, magisterium. Definitions can be found in this guide's glossary.
- Be prepared to answer questions about Church authority as it relates to sacred Tradition.
- Gather some soft background music for the guided meditation.

Welcome

Greet the participants and check for supplies and immediate needs. Solicit questions or comments about the previous session and/or share any new information. Begin promptly.

Opening Scripture

John 16:13–15

Light the candle and read the passage aloud. Allow for a moment of silence, and then welcome any comments or reactions. Begin to discuss the topics of divine revelation and Church authority by asking two questions: "What have you heard about God or the Catholic Church? How do you know whether or not it is true?"

"The People of God as a whole never ceases to welcome, to penetrate more deeply, and to live more fully from the gift of divine Revelation." CCC 99

In Short:

- God reveals himself to us and to the world.
- God reveals himself through many means.
- God wants us to know him fully and clearly.

Divine Revelation

Think back to when you started a special friendship. As your relationship developed, you revealed more of yourself—thoughts and feelings, likes and dislikes, hopes and dreams. Over time, your friend came to have a pretty good sense of *who you are.* Yet as close as you may be, no other person can claim to understand you completely. We continue to discover and reveal new aspects of ourselves as we move through life.

We can apply some of these same relationship principles to how God reveals himself to us. Remember that God is a loving communion of persons—three divine persons in one God. God is loving relationship and provides a model for how we, who are created in his image, are to live—in relationship with God and the community of his Church.

Our Universal Desire for God

Throughout time, people have longed for and sought union with God. This drive to know God is reflected in various writings from our tradition:

- "My soul longs for you, O God" (Psalm 42:2).
- "Our hearts are restless till they find rest in You" (St. Augustine, *Confessions,* 1.1).
- "The desire for God is written in the human heart, because man is created by God and for God" (*CCC* 27).
- Blaise Pascal—mathematician, physicist, and theologian—wrote of a God-shaped hole in the heart of every person that can only be filled by God as made known through Jesus Christ.

- *Which of the above best fits your experience of seeking and being sought by God?*

Creation and Human Experience

We can find God in his creation of the universe. In seascapes and star fields, in woodland hikes, in animals, and in the deep emotions we feel for other people, we find evidence of an all-knowing, all-loving Creator.

As "wonderfully made" human persons, we also find God through our human nature and experience (Psalm 139:14). We have a soul and are designed to seek truth, beauty, and happiness. In creating us, God grants us freedom, consciences, and the use of reason to guide us. The more we become aware of ourselves and our relationship to God, the more convinced we'll be that God is present and offers us wholeness and real satisfaction.

CCC 27–100

ADULTS

Divine Revelation

Remind participants that despite God's desire to reveal himself fully, in this world there will always remain mysteries. Only in heaven will we see God, ourselves, and the world as they are. To accept a teaching or reality without understanding is an assent of *faith,* a humble acceptance of our human position, and praiseworthy. Allow the group to respond, discuss, and offer personal examples.

Explain that there are two ways we come to know God: human intellect and reason (understanding the created world and other people) and divine revelation (Scripture and sacred Tradition).

Reinforce logic and reason's role in revealing God: explain that our uniquely human ability to "figure things out" is not in opposition to, but *cooperates with,* God's saving work. The Church asserts that science and faith can coexist; many faithful Catholics are scientists or use science to bring the kingdom to others. We can't discover or "create" anything that God can't use to reveal his truth for our benefit.

Creation and Human Experience

Read aloud this quote from the *Catechism,* then allow participants to respond: "In different ways, man can come to know that there exists a reality which is the first cause and final end of all things, a reality that everyone calls 'God'" (*CCC* 34).

Have participants share their responses to the lesson's question, "Where do you experience God?" Then offer examples from each of these four ways (31–38, 54–67):

- *The world* — nature and the cosmos, including the sciences (laws of physics).
- *The human person* — personal desires, experiences, relationships, and abilities (deducing higher truths and meanings for life and self).
- *Scripture* — protection of Israelites and fulfillment of prophecies in Old Testament, life and resurrection of Jesus in New Testament.
- *Sacred Tradition* — papal and magisterial documents.

Divine Revelation in Scripture

Read aloud this quote from the *Catechism*, which reinforces the basic understanding of divine revelation:

"By natural reason man can know God with certainty, on the basis of his works. But there is another order of knowledge, which man cannot possibly arrive at by his own powers: the order of divine Revelation. Through an utterly free decision, God has revealed himself and given himself to man. This he does by revealing the mystery, his plan of loving goodness, formed from all eternity in Christ, for the benefit of all men. God has fully revealed this plan by sending us his beloved Son, our Lord Jesus Christ, and the Holy Spirit."

CCC 50

Divine Revelation in Sacred Tradition

Encourage participants who were raised without religion or who struggle with religious authority to grow in their trust of the Church's role in helping them encounter God: "The Church is catholic: she proclaims the fullness of the faith. She bears in herself and administers the totality of the means of salvation" (*CCC* 868).

Remind them, if necessary, that prior to having a formal Scripture, many books and writings in the Bible underwent generations of oral tradition. Other events and truths about Jesus were shared among the disciples but never written down.

"Ever since the creation of the world, [God's] invisible attributes of eternal power and divinity have been able to be understood and perceived in what he has made."

Romans 1:20

- *Where do you experience God—in the rhythms of nature, a loving friend, the wonders of space?*

Divine Revelation in Scripture

God didn't just create the world and leave us to our own devices (CCC 50). Our Creator communicates his love and will to us, for us. This is important, because there are moral and religious truths that reason and intelligence alone cannot fully grasp.

Divine revelation is God's making himself and his saving plan known to us. Just as we reveal our hearts to a friend, God shares his will with us and invites us to friendship.

God reveals himself and his plan *within history and to people.* From Adam, Eve, and Noah to St. Paul and the early Church, sacred Scripture contains the inspired and inerrant witness to God's presence, actions, and saving works.

Jesus is the full revelation of God, the Word of God made flesh who "made his dwelling among us" (John 1:14). Jesus is the historical and human "face of God" and mediator between God and all humankind.

In fact, "all the Scriptures—the Law, the Prophets, and the Psalms—are fulfilled in Christ" (*CCC* 2763, see Luke 24:44). This revelation was present in a veiled way in the Old Testament but made explicit in the New Testament (*CCC* 65–67). In the fullness of time, God's plan is revealed through Christ's ministry, death, resurrection, ascension, and Second Coming. Through Jesus, all can encounter God and be saved.

"In this way the love of God was revealed to us: God sent his only Son into the world so that we might have life through him. In this is love: not that we have loved God, but that he loved us and sent his Son as expiation for our sins."

1 John 4:9–10

"[God] wills everyone to be saved and to come to knowledge of the truth."

1 Timothy 2:4

- *Has the Spirit ever presented a Bible passage to you at a timely moment? Does a certain verse or figure resonate with you? If so, write it down and display it in a prominent place so you can revisit it often, perhaps even memorize it.*
- *What difference does it make that God became one of us in Jesus?*

Divine Revelation in Sacred Tradition

As Jesus' life on earth was coming to an end, he instructed his apostles to continue his mission of sharing the good news of God's love and the promise of eternal life. He sent them the Holy Spirit to be their helper and guide. With the Spirit's assistance, the apostles witnessed to, preached, and wrote about the revelation of God, rooted in Jesus' words and actions. They made sure the gospel was handed on intact.

The Spirit also guided and assisted the apostles in choosing successors and handing on to them "what they received from Jesus' teaching and example and what they learned from the Holy Spirit" (CCC 83). So, beginning with Jesus, the line of authentic, Spirit-filled transmission of divine revelation continues through the apostles' successors: the popes and bishops. The Church's ongoing teaching, rooted in the **apostolic tradition** but not recorded in Scripture, is called **sacred Tradition** (note the capital T).

> *"Go, therefore, and make disciples of all nations, baptizing them in the name of the Father, and of the Son, and of the holy Spirit, teaching them to observe all that I have commanded you. And behold, I am with you always, until the end of the age."*
>
> Matthew 28:19–20

> *"The Advocate, the holy Spirit that the Father will send in my name—he will teach you everything and remind you of all that [I] told you."*
>
> John 14:26

Scripture *and* Tradition

The Bible is a major and special part of the apostolic tradition, and the Church is rooted, nourished, and ruled by Scripture. The Catholic Church's teaching voice, the **magisterium**, was engaged before there was a New Testament. Today, the magisterium applies biblical teachings to new situations for each generation. Because we believe that the Church continues to be inspired by the Holy Spirit, these teachings become part of sacred Tradition, part of God's divine revelation to us. When new questions of faith and morality emerge, the Spirit guides the Church to discern Christ's will. The Church guides its members in right living, making Christ's teachings clear to them.

> *"You are Peter, and upon this rock I will build my church, and the gates of the netherworld shall not prevail against it. I will give you the keys to the kingdom of heaven. Whatever you bind on earth shall be bound in heaven; and whatever you loose on earth shall be loosed in heaven."*
>
> Matthew 16:18–20

Core or Custom?

Through Scripture and sacred Tradition, God has revealed what we need to know for the sake of our salvation. We include in Tradition (big T) those truths that are core to Christianity. However, there are many traditions (small t) that aren't necessary for our salvation and so aren't part of (big T) Tradition. For example, the resurrection of Jesus Christ is core to our Tradition. The rosary is a prayer that enables us to meditate on the core truths of faith, but in itself is not part of sacred Tradition. It's important to distinguish between what's core and what's not, what's necessary for our salvation and what's a cherished practice ("Scripture and Tradition: Revealing God's Plan," Margaret Nutting Ralph, PhD).

Life contains many distractions and obstacles. A person's path to God is seldom straight and smooth. Yet here you are. God is present in your life and has led you to this moment. We can miss out on many wonderful things if we don't pay attention to the truth and signs around us. Ask the Spirit to show you God's hand in all of your experiences.

- *What have been the greatest challenges to your life and faith?*
- *What opened your heart to seek God and truth?*

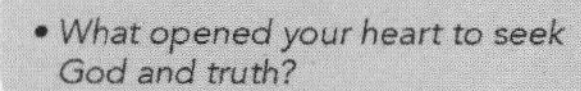

Core or Custom?

Place some Catholic teachings or practices (perhaps ones participants already have questions or concerns about) in this context to provide some perspective. Enlist the assistance of the pastor and/or other authoritative resources.

Suggested topics may include ritual/sacramental norms vs. liturgical styles, Marian dogma vs. specific devotions or apparitions, or papal infallibility vs. pastoral guidance.

Emphasize that conversion and initiation need not be hindered or delayed by "small t" traditions, whereas "big T" Tradition should be generally understood and accepted. If any participants have serious doubts about "big T" dogma or doctrine, encourage them to keep seeking and to discuss the matter with the pastor. Keep this discussion brief and on topic. Address personal matters privately.

Scripture *and* Tradition

Read and share excerpts from the Dogmatic Constitution on Divine Revelation (*Dei Verbum*), a Vatican II document, for an authoritative discussion on the relationship between Scripture and Tradition.

Ask participants who struggle with this teaching and cling to a "Bible only" perspective, "What would happen if the Bible were translated into a number of native languages and given to people who knew nothing about God apart from the translation you give them?" Imagine going back years later to study their faith, practices, and beliefs. Would a Bible-only approach yield the same results in every group? As Catholics, we believe that the Holy Spirit leads the Church into truth and that both Scripture *and* Tradition are necessary to carry on the gospel mission.

Guided Meditation

Provide some time for the reflection questions, then read the meditation prompts aloud prayerfully, pausing after each one. Don't force anyone who is uncomfortable or resistant to participate. Soft background music, mood lighting, and flexible seating arrangements are helpful.

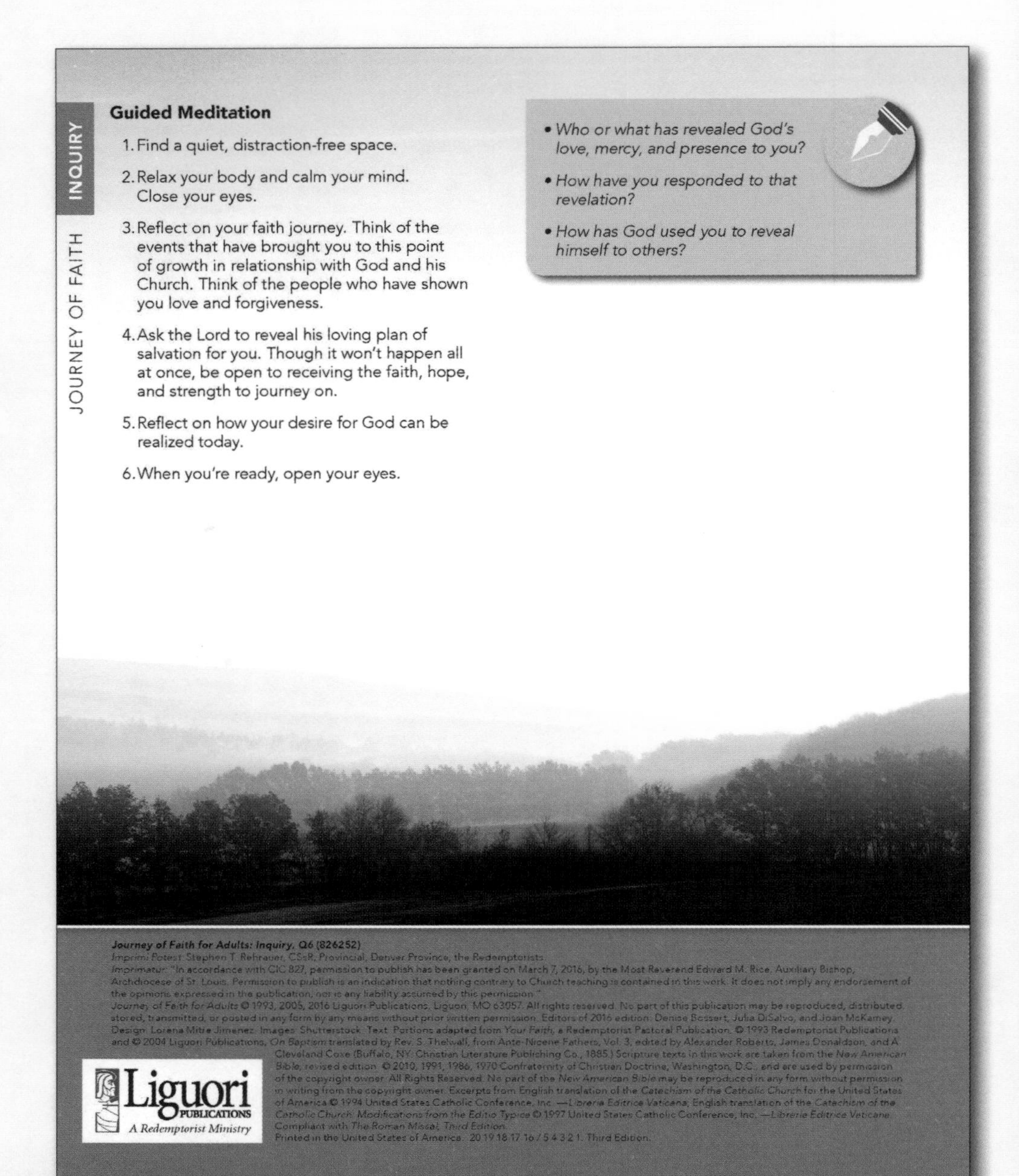

JOURNEY OF FAITH INQUIRY

Guided Meditation

1. Find a quiet, distraction-free space.
2. Relax your body and calm your mind. Close your eyes.
3. Reflect on your faith journey. Think of the events that have brought you to this point of growth in relationship with God and his Church. Think of the people who have shown you love and forgiveness.
4. Ask the Lord to reveal his loving plan of salvation for you. Though it won't happen all at once, be open to receiving the faith, hope, and strength to journey on.
5. Reflect on how your desire for God can be realized today.
6. When you're ready, open your eyes.

- *Who or what has revealed God's love, mercy, and presence to you?*
- *How have you responded to that revelation?*
- *How has God used you to reveal himself to others?*

Journey of Faith for Adults: Inquiry, Q6 (826252)
Imprimi Potest: Stephen T. Rehrauer, CSsR, Provincial, Denver Province, the Redemptorists.
Imprimatur: "In accordance with CIC 827, permission to publish has been granted on March 7, 2016, by the Most Reverend Edward M. Rice, Auxiliary Bishop, Archdiocese of St. Louis. Permission to publish is an indication that nothing contrary to Church teaching is contained in this work. It does not imply any endorsement of the opinions expressed in the publication; nor is any liability assumed by this permission."

Printed in the United States of America. 20 19 18 17 16 / 5 4 3 2 1. Third Edition.

Journaling

Invite participants to reflect on the many ways God reveals himself to the world. They may respond to the three questions in their journal.

Closing Prayer

Read aloud this prayer of St. Augustine (*CCC* 30):

You are great, O Lord, and greatly to be praised: great is your power and your wisdom is without measure. And man, so small a part of your creation, wants to praise you: this man, though clothed with mortality and bearing the evidence of sin and the proof that you withstand the proud. Despite everything, man, though but a small part of your creation, wants to praise you. You yourself encourage him to delight in your praise, for you have made us for yourself, and our heart is restless until it rests in you (see Confessions, Book 1, Chapter 1).

Looking Ahead

Lesson Q7 *Your Prayer Life* introduces prayer as communication with God and opening oneself to his revelation. Encourage everyone to find and practice a comfortable Christian prayer form or text this week.

Q7: Your Prayer Life

Catechism: 2558–69, 2598–2616, 2626–49, 2653–54, 2659–60, 2691, 2697–2745

Objectives

Participants will...

- describe prayer as communication with God.
- recall and practice basic forms and styles of Christian prayer.
- recognize prayer as both a communal and personal action.

Leader Meditation

John 16:23–27; Matthew 18:19–20

These passages teach us something important about the power of prayer. Which modes of prayer are most comfortable for you? Consider spending as much time in prayer as you do in preparation for lessons. Saint Teresa of Calcutta once was asked how she and her sisters could spend so much time in prayer when there was so much to do. "If we don't take time to pray, we could not do this work," she said simply.

Related *Catholic Updates*

- "An Invitation to Prayer" (C9202A)
- "Stealing Moments of Quiet: Finding God in Prayer" (C1505A)

Leader Preparation

- Read the lesson, this lesson plan, the Scripture passages, and the *Catechism* sections.
- Be familiar with the terms: prayer, eucharistic adoration, pilgrimage, *lectio divina*. Definitions can be found in this guide's glossary.
- Gather or prepare some prayers for the group, but keep your participants' comfort levels in mind. This lesson's focus is on understanding what prayer is (and *isn't*) and on communicating with God in new ways. The next lesson details traditional Catholic prayers and practices.
- Consider the prayer resources available to your group—special locations, ministries, libraries, events—and gather information on them as they pertain to your participants.

Welcome

Greet each person as he or she arrives. Check for supplies and immediate needs. Solicit questions or comments about the previous session and/or share new information and findings. Begin promptly.

Opening Scripture

John 16:23–27; Matthew 18:19–20

Light the candle and read the passages aloud. Allow for a moment of silence, and then welcome any comments or reactions to the readings. Ask the participants, "What is the purpose and goal of any prayer?" Acknowledge their responses—in truth, there are many reasons to pray, and all come to God with their own intentions. Point out that, ultimately, all sincere prayer leads us closer to the Trinity and strengthens our love for God and others.

> "Where does prayer come from? Whether prayer is expressed in words or gestures, it is the whole man who prays. But in naming the source of prayer, Scripture speaks sometimes of the soul or the spirit, but most often of the heart (more than a thousand times)."
>
> CCC 2562

Q7

INQUIRY

In Short:

- Prayer is communicating with God.
- Prayer has many forms and styles.
- We can pray alone or in a group.

Your Prayer Life

We've come to know and believe that God made us, loves us, and longs to be in relationship with us. But we can't have a relationship with someone we never talk to. Our faith has to become personal. Prayer helps make it personal.

What Is Prayer?

Prayer has a pretty broad definition. It's really anything we do that brings us into conversation with God. It can be a conversation, a common prayer like the Our Father, or any experience that makes you feel closer to God. We can pray to God when we want to praise him, we can petition God when we need something, or we can give thanks to God for something good.

"I have called you by name: you are mine."

Isaiah 43:1

How Do I Start?

Prayer begins in the heart; it is "the place of encounter...the place of covenant" (CCC 2563). You know how it feels to let someone into your heart; invite Jesus to meet you there, too. It can begin as simply as saying "hello": *I'm here, God. I'm ready to talk and to listen.* Just showing up and agreeing to enter the conversation is an act of faith and love. Maybe you just want to sit and talk about what's on your mind. It doesn't matter if your prayer is deep, serious, lighthearted, long, or short. God meets you wherever you are.

*"**Prayer** is the raising of one's mind and heart to God or the requesting of good things from God."*

St. John Damascene; CCC 2559

What if God Doesn't Respond?

God is *always* present and listening, but we're not always aware of it—or of his response. Sometimes we focus so much on our words and needs and how we're praying that we forget about God. *Let go of expectations.* God's answers don't always come in the way or on the timeline we envision. As life passes, listen for hints in conversations or in what you're reading and watching. Maybe a sentence, image, or person will touch your heart with particular clarity. Maybe your feelings will begin to change. There might not be an immediate or obvious answer, but God *will* respond.

CCC 2558–69, 2598–2616, 2626–49, 2653–54, 2659–60, 2691, 2697–2745

ADULTS

Q7

What Is Prayer?

Remind participants that God wants us to share anything and everything with him, just as he shares himself with us. Discuss how a life of prayer establishes and sustains this loving relationship.

Ask candidates and sponsors to give examples of their prayer practices and how it deepens their relationship with Christ.

How Do I Start?

Point out that every participant has prayed before—even if he or she doesn't know it. In the RCIA process, they will gain greater awareness of their communications with God and practice new and different kinds of prayer. Their reflections on Scripture, closing prayers, and use of their prayer journals are all examples of prayer.

Can I Pray "Wrong?"

Ask participants, "Do you think there are right and wrong ways to pray?" Invite them to offer examples, and acknowledge their responses.

Clarify that in personal prayer, some "wrong" ways to pray might be to pray with selfish intentions, to feign (fake) opening ourselves to God, or to worship another "deity" or idol out of spite. In communal (group) prayer, such as during a Mass liturgy, the words and formulas are prescribed, but honest mistakes are never sinful. Printed guides (like missalettes) and others will guide and support you.

Kinds of Prayer

Review each kind of prayer listed in this lesson and have participants discuss which methods intrigue them and why. If they have a current or favorite prayer style not listed here, determine which category it may fit into. Encourage them to explore and reflect on their prayer preferences.

Invite the group, including team leaders and sponsors, to share their response to the question, "Where do you get away…?"

Mention any relevant prayer resources available to participants and encourage them to take advantage of them. Point out that the next lesson, *Q8 Catholic Prayers and Practices*, will discuss some of these in greater detail.

Can I Pray "Wrong?"

Our prayer experiences won't always be the same. Sometimes they will be deep; sometimes they will feel dull or flat. Isn't that the way it is with most things?

Don't worry about praying the "right" way. Don't get discouraged. Speak openly and honestly to God—even if that means bringing your unattractive or unpopular parts with you. God can handle our bad attitudes and mistakes.

Kinds of Prayer

> *"Christian Tradition has retained three major expressions of prayer: vocal, meditative, and contemplative."*
>
> CCC 2699

1. *Vocal prayer* includes private conversations and group expressions of praise and petition. It can be informal, spontaneous, traditional (Our Father), or liturgical (the Mass).
2. In *meditative prayer*, we reflect on something—often the Scriptures, a spiritual writing, or life events—in order to open our heart to God's will. Common examples are *lectio divina* (page 3) and the rosary.
3. *Contemplative prayer* allows the Spirit to draw us into our own hearts. Its key components are finding a quiet place, asking God to guide and bless our contemplation, and being mindful of our breathing. As we pray, we might focus on a single word, image, or short prayer.

Within these categories, there are countless forms and styles. Try one of the prayers in this lesson, or find your own.

Pray With Nature
Go to a park, lake, garden, or zoo. Visit a nearby stream, field, or grove. Climb a mountain. Make it a journey *to* and *with* God. Remind yourself of the magnificence of his creation. Cultivate a sense of wonder, awe, and mystery.

- *Where do you get away from life's demands? Is there a place that you find especially peaceful? Consider turning this place into a special prayer space.*

Visit a Holy Place
You don't have to wait for Sunday to go to church. God is always present there. Many parishes also have chapels for **Eucharistic Adoration**—a "holy hour" of prayer and worship to Jesus in the Eucharist that takes place outside of Mass.

A **pilgrimage** is a "journey to a sacred place undertaken as an act of religious devotion" (*Modern Catholic Dictionary*). Whether the place is near or far, you are pursuing God, and the physical journey itself becomes a prayer. This tradition appears in the Old Testament. God's people have always been a pilgrim people—on a journey to the holy, to God.

Pray Using Imagery
Saint Ignatius of Loyola bases much of his teaching about spiritual life on imagery. He recommends reading a Scripture passage slowly, especially stories about Jesus, picturing scenes in your mind, and imagining yourself in them. Let the story unfold with both Jesus and you present.

Pray With Scripture
The Church encourages "frequent reading of the divine Scriptures….Prayer should accompany the reading of Sacred Scripture, so that a dialogue takes place between God and man. For 'we speak to him when we pray; we listen to him when we read' the [Scriptures]" (*CCC* 2653).

As you discuss holy places, direct participants to your parish's adoration chapel, if it has one, or to any nearby shrine or retreat center. Display images and share its history or mission, if there's time. Offer details and directions to anyone interested.

One ancient Catholic practice is called ***lectio divina***, or divine reading. Read a Scripture passage slowly and savor little bits of it. Often a word or phrase will stand out, or the scene will take on new life or meaning.

The writings of the saints can also lead our hearts deeper into prayer and closer to God. As we read the writings of holy people, we sense God's nearness. That experience can transform us.

Write Your Prayer
Journaling is another way to express our thoughts and feelings toward God. When we feel spiritually dry, it can be helpful to reread something we wrote at a more vibrant point in our faith journey. It reminds us that God is always faithful, listening, and present. Jesus seems to say, "Remember when...?"

Sing Your Prayer
Saint Augustine is attributed with saying, "He who sings prays twice." Sing familiar and favorite songs, or compose your own melody and lyrics. God doesn't care about pitch or vocal quality. If you sing from your heart, it's prayer! Playing an instrument can be prayer as well.

Pray With Your Body
Catholics kneel, fold their hands, bow, and much more. If you don't know what to say, convey a message in gesture—lift your hands, bow your head, raise your face, or dance! We communicate with others through touch and body language all the time. Sometimes, words aren't necessary.

Pray in Silence
In our busy lives, we can forget the value of simply being with God. It takes deliberate intention to seek him. At first, this prayer may last only a few seconds, but with practice, the time will lengthen. You can make—or find—these times throughout the day. Eventually, you'll discover that you can "pray without ceasing" (1 Thessalonians 5:17).

Pray When You're "Too Busy" to Pray
Busy lives mean we pray on the go, in the midst of daily life. Say a prayer as you get dressed in the morning, as you think about your kids during the day, or as you avoid a traffic accident on the drive home. While it's good to make regular time for prayer, it's also good to connect with God throughout your day.

Offer It Up
In the face of a challenge, dilemma, or trial, patiently enduring any suffering or accepting a minor sacrifice can become a prayerful offering of hope and faith in Christ, who redeems the world. Our suffering and sacrifice unites us to Christ as we recall his suffering and death that won our salvation.

Give Thanks in Prayer
We can make thankfulness the centerpiece of our prayer and life. Every evening, we can thank God for at least one thing we've never thought to thank God for before. The word *Eucharist* means "thanksgiving" or "grateful" in Greek; the Mass is our communal *way of giving thanks* to God. Cultivate an attitude of gratitude in your life.

Pray the News
Praying for others is as important as praying for ourselves. Choose a person or situation in the news, giving thanks for the good and requesting help for those in need. Besides countering any negative or false messages, this prayer connects us to the world and prompts us to appropriate action.

Pray the "Jesus Prayer"
Lord Jesus Christ, Son of God, have mercy on me, a sinner.

Some Final Tips

Ask, "What 'works' for you when it comes to prayer? What helps you to enter a prayerful state and maintain your focus?" Consider incorporating some of these suggestions into your prayers during the sessions.

Invite team members and sponsors to share any additional advice that hasn't yet been mentioned.

INQUIRY

JOURNEY OF FAITH

Some Final Tips

- *Minimize distractions.* If you need to adjust location, position, lighting, temperature, or noise level to focus on God—and you're able to do so easily—do it.
- *Be patient yet diligent.* If your mind wanders, gently return your attention to God, your prayer word(s), Scripture passage, or the concern at hand. If you get out of the habit, just start again. While in the moment, pause for a while. Does anything else emerge? Is there something Jesus wants to say to you?
- *Keep it simple.* Don't try to say, do, or figure out too much. Whenever a prayer comes to you, let it out.
- *Don't force it.* Don't go through the motions for the sake of habit or accomplishment. If a prayer is no longer working, try something new. Just keep praying.
- *Don't answer for God.* Prayer isn't an order form for a perfect life. In responding to God's call, make yourself vulnerable to his ways.

Practice one of the prayers listed in this lesson, then describe your experience in your journal.

***Journey of Faith for Adults: Inquiry*, Q7 (826252)**
Imprimi Potest: Stephen T. Rehrauer, CSsR, Provincial, Denver Province, the Redemptorists
Imprimatur: "In accordance with CIC 827, permission to publish has been granted on March 7, 2016, by the Most Reverend Edward M. Rice, Auxiliary Bishop, Archdiocese of St. Louis. Permission to publish is an indication that nothing contrary to Church teaching is contained in this work. It does not imply any endorsement of the opinions expressed in the publication; nor is any liability assumed by this permission."

Text: Some prayer suggestions adapted from *Six Ways to Perk Up Your Prayer Life*. Excerpts from *Modern Catholic Dictionary* by Fr. John A. Hardon, SJ © Eternal Life. Editors of 2016 edition: Denise Bossert, Julia DiSalvo, and Joan McKamey. Design: Lorena Mitre Jimenez. Images: Shutterstock.

Printed in the United States of America. 20 19 18 17 16 / 5 4 3 2 1. Third Edition

Liguori PUBLICATIONS
A Redemptorist Ministry

Journaling

Remind participants to practice one of the prayer forms in this lesson sometime this week. Consider giving time for sharing and follow-up questions in the next session.

Closing Prayer

Go around the room and allow each (willing) participant to speak a spontaneous prayer of praise or thanksgiving. Encourage the mentioning of any special intentions. If time is limited or the group is too large, confine it to the RCIA team leaders.

Looking Ahead

Lesson *Q8 Catholic Prayers and Practices* introduces participants to traditional Catholic prayers, specifically those of the rosary, and to the Catholic culture of prayer. In their exploration of prayer this week, have participants observe or practice a uniquely Catholic prayer form in addition to the one they select for journaling.

Q8: Catholic Prayers and Practices

Catechism: 167, 170–171, 971, 1174–78, 2650–51, 2675–79, 2759–76

Objectives

Participants will…

- recognize that having a variety of prayers *and* common, traditional (standard) prayers meet the needs of the faithful and keep them in unity with each other and with God.
- recite the major prayers and recall the mysteries of the rosary.
- practice another traditional Catholic prayer (form).

Leader Meditation

Acts 2:42–47

This passage provides a glimpse into the way the Church's traditions began. Many people return to the Church because they miss the traditions and rituals that bonded them to Christ and the community. Meditate on what it means to be Catholic, then answer this question to yourself: "If I weren't Catholic, which traditions would I miss most? What prayers and practices connect me to Jesus and his living body?"

Read the passage again, focusing on verse 47: The disciples praised God, and he "added to their number" daily. Do the same now: Praise God for your participants and pray that God will add to your numbers.

Related *Catholic Updates*

- "The Rosary: A Prayer for All Seasons" (C0308A)
- "Liturgy of the Hours: Sharing Your Day With God" (C1312A)
- "Eucharistic Adoration: Drawing Closer to Jesus" (C1206B)
- "The Sacramentals: Embracing God Through Creation" (C9307A)

Leader Preparation

- Read the lesson, this lesson plan, the Scripture passage, and the *Catechism* sections. Review these related lessons if necessary: *Q7 Your Prayer Life, Q14 Mary, E4 The Creed*, and *E6 The Lord's Prayer.*
- Be familiar with the terms: hallowed, amen, creed, chaplet, rosary, Liturgy of the Hours (Divine Office), novena, Angelus, Benediction of the Blessed Sacrament, monstrance, genuflection, litany, icon, sacramental. Definitions can be found in this guide's glossary.
- Be prepared to discuss the history of the Hail Mary and the rosary. If your parish has a rosary group, approach them about providing a rosary for each participant. Liguori offers *Let's Pray (Not Just Say) the Rosary* to anyone seeking a step-by-step, Scripture-based resource on this popular devotion. Strongly consider purchasing copies for all your participants and sponsors.
- Gather items to talk about: a copy of the Creed (in the *Catechism*), breviary, rosary, monstrance, and other items. Ask team members and sponsors to bring in their favorite sacramentals or Catholic prayer helps. If possible, take a trip to the adoration chapel or schedule a guest speaker from one of the parish's prayer ministries. Consider other Catholic prayers: St. Francis' Peace prayer, St. Patrick's Breastplate, the Memorare, the Chaplet of Divine Mercy, or others.

Welcome

Greet each person with the same words—perhaps with "the Lord be with you" if they are familiar with the liturgy—to model the value of traditional prayers. Check for supplies and immediate needs. Solicit questions or comments about the previous session and/or share new information and findings. Begin promptly.

Opening Scripture

Acts 2:42–47

After lighting the candle, read the passage aloud. Talk about the mission of the Church and how guiding prayer is an integral part of that mission. If there's time, note other sacred traditions that have their roots in the early Church—the breaking of bread (Eucharist/Mass) and emphasis on shared teaching and living.

> "Prayer cannot be reduced to the spontaneous outpouring of interior impulse….The tradition of Christian prayer is one of the ways in which the tradition of faith takes shape and grows, especially through the contemplation and study of believers."
>
> CCC 2650–51; see *Dei Verbum*, 8

Q8

INQUIRY

In Short:

- We connect to God through personal and traditional prayers.
- The rosary reflects the mystery of Christ.
- There are many traditional Catholic prayers to try.

Catholic Prayers and Practices

Sometimes we can't find the words to pray. We may feel overwhelmed or unable to concentrate. In those moments, having prayers committed to memory is helpful. *Repeating a prayer can focus our attention on God and quiet our minds.*

Catholics repeat some prayers because we've found they're the best way to express certain thoughts to God. You may frequently say, "I love you" to your family because these are the simplest and clearest words to convey how you feel.

Memorizing prayers makes it easier to pray with others. When we pray together, we both express and enhance our sense of community.

- *What effects and advantages of praying with other people do you see?*

These basic prayers may be used alone or in combination with other Catholic prayers and rites.

The Our Father (The Lord's Prayer)

Our Father, who art in heaven, hallowed be thy name; thy kingdom come; thy will be done on earth as it is in heaven. Give us this day our daily bread; and forgive us our trespasses as we forgive those who trespass against us; and lead us not into temptation, but deliver us from evil. Amen.

Matthew 6:9–15 and Luke 11:1–4

This is the best-known prayer of Christianity, probably because it's the one Jesus taught his disciples when one of them said, "Lord, teach us to pray" (Luke 11:1). We are the adopted daughters and sons of God, and so we can call God "Father." We don't pray for ourselves alone but for everyone as members of God's family.

As children of God, we want to honor God. **Hallowed** means to "make holy"; we want God's name to be honored by all, and we want God's desire for humanity to be fulfilled. All that Jesus did and taught was the will of God. We pray that we may have help and strength to do God's will. And God's will is for us to have life and to have it fully (John 10:10).

Although spiritually Christ himself is our "bread of life," our daily bread for our life and faith journey, we ask God for all we need to live each day (John 6:35, 48). That includes forgiveness for the wrongs we have done. We recognize our sinfulness and acknowledge God's merciful love and forgiveness. If we hope for forgiveness from God, we must be willing to forgive others. Finally, we pray to be kept safe from the power of evil and all that leads to evil.

CCC 167, 170–171, 971, 1174–78, 2650–51, 2675–79, 2759–76

ADULTS

Q8

Catholic Prayers and Practices

Ask the lesson's question out loud: "What effects and advantages of praying with other people do you see?" Invite participants to share their thoughts with the group.

Point out that while all prayers are beneficial, the Church does put greater weight on prayers from Scripture, saints, and the Church, given their closeness to God. This doesn't contradict the previous lesson or dismiss any individual prayer style. Rather, it honors the revelation and authority given by God for the good of all.

Mention that future lessons—Q9, Q14, and Q15 specifically—will discuss the Mass and intercessory prayer, two major forms of Catholic prayer. Once participants begin attending Mass and Adoration, demonstrate the proper way to genuflect before a tabernacle or monstrance.

The Our Father (The Lord's Prayer)

Model the four "traditional" prayers out loud, perhaps with team members and sponsors. Remind them that lesson E4 will give a detailed study of the Nicene Creed and E6 on the Lord's Prayer.

Connect these prayers with the three expressions in the previous lesson—vocal, meditative, contemplative—by explaining that when prayed within the context of a public liturgy, the prayer is *vocal*. When spoken out loud, it may also be *vocal* prayer. But if prayed silently, even if led aloud by an individual or group, the prayer is *meditative*. The rosary is given as an example of meditative prayer in lesson Q7.

You'll learn more about the Lord's Prayer in a later lesson.

- *What might it mean to accept God as your "father?" How can prayer help you live out this decision?*

The Sign of the Cross

In the name of the Father, and of the Son, and of the Holy Spirit. Amen.

This blessing dates to the second century when Christians would trace a cross on their foreheads with their thumbs. The gesture is used in the anointing that's a part of baptism and confirmation.

The Sign of the Cross prayer is made by touching the fingertips of your right hand to your forehead, breast, left shoulder, then right shoulder. The gesture is accompanied by the words of the prayer honoring the Trinity. It's the traditional way Catholics begin and end our prayers. We also end most prayers by saying, "**Amen**," which means, "Yes; I believe."

The Hail Mary

Hail Mary, full of grace, the Lord is with you;
blessed are you among women,
and blessed is the fruit of your womb, Jesus.
Holy Mary, Mother of God,
pray for us sinners
now and at the hour of our death.
Amen.

The Hail Mary begins with two biblical verses: the words of the Archangel Gabriel—"Hail, favored one! The Lord is with you"—and of Mary's cousin Elizabeth—"Most blessed are you among women, and blessed is the fruit of your womb" (Luke 1:28, 42). It concludes with a request that acknowledges Mary as the Mother of our Savior. In this prayer, we don't worship Mary; only God is worthy of our worship. We join God in honoring Mary because of her special relationship to Jesus and pray to be able to follow her example of surrendering to God's will.

The Apostles' Creed

I believe in God,
the Father almighty,
Creator of heaven and earth,
and in Jesus Christ, his only Son, our Lord,
who was conceived by the Holy Spirit, born of the Virgin Mary,
suffered under Pontius Pilate,
was crucified, died and was buried;
he descended into hell;
on the third day he rose again from the dead;
he ascended into heaven,
and is seated at the right hand of God the Father almighty;
from there he will come to judge the living and the dead.
I believe in the Holy Spirit,
the holy catholic Church,
the communion of saints,
the forgiveness of sins,
the resurrection of the body,
and life everlasting.
Amen.

The Apostles' Creed "is rightly considered to be a faithful summary of the apostles' faith" (*CCC* 194). From the Latin for "I believe," our **creed** is a basic statement of Christian belief and an instrument of Church unity. It's most often recited at Mass or as part of a **chaplet**.

Chaplet: "Beads strung together on which prayers are counted as they are recited," such as a rosary; also, the series of prayers recited on such beads (*Modern Catholic Dictionary*).

The Rosary

The **rosary** is a meditation on the events (called "mysteries") in the life of Jesus and Mary. There are four sets, each including five mysteries: the Joyful Mysteries, the Sorrowful Mysteries, the Glorious Mysteries, and the Luminous Mysteries.

The rosary is an excellent everyday prayer and is especially useful when we want to pray but find it difficult or impossible to pray in our own words. For many Catholics, the rosary offers great comfort in difficult times.

1. Make the sign of the cross and say the Apostles' Creed.
2. Say the Lord's Prayer.
3. Say three Hail Marys.
4. Say the Glory Be and announce the first mystery.
5. Say the Lord's Prayer.
6. Say ten Hail Marys while meditating on the mystery.
7. Repeat steps 4, 5, and 6, continuing with the second, third, fourth, and fifth mysteries.

Other Catholic Prayers and Devotions

The **Liturgy of the Hours** (or **Divine Office**) is a repeating cycle of prayers, hymns, and readings for various "hours" of the day—up to a total of seven. *Hours* refers to how the prayers mark the phases of the day, *not* how long each prayer lasts. This is part of the daily, public prayer of the Church; the other part is the Mass.

Novena, from the Latin word meaning "nine," refers to a devotion that extends for nine consecutive days (weeks or months). The set number was originally based on the apostles' nine days of prayer between the ascension of Jesus and the Spirit's coming at Pentecost.

The **Angelus** is a prayer recounting the events that led up to our Lord's birth and our redemption. It is recited at 6 AM, noon, and 6 PM.

Benediction of the Blessed Sacrament is the prayerful ceremony in which a host of the Eucharist is exposed for adoration in a **monstrance**.

Genuflection—bending the knee as a sign of reverence for the presence of Christ in the Eucharist.

Litany—literally a "list" of saints. After each saint is named, we sing or say, "Pray for us."

INQUIRY

JOURNEY OF FAITH

Other Catholic Prayers and Devotions

Ask participants if they have questions about any Catholic practices they have seen or heard about. Much misinformation exists regarding our traditions and beliefs. Don't hesitate to say you don't know the answer to a question. Let the participant know you will find out and follow up.

The Rosary

Distribute copies of a rosary resource to participants (see above) and use it during this or a subsequent session. This lesson doesn't mention the *Fatima prayer*, but *Let's Pray (Not Just Say) the Rosary* does.

Sacramentals

Display or pass around some sacramentals or prayer items, if there's time. Identify each one and explain where it came from and/or how it's used. If it's a personal belonging, have the owner share its meaning or significance.

JOURNEY OF FAITH | INQUIRY

Sacramentals

Sacramentals are visible signs that draw us to God and make all aspects of life holy. A common part of Catholic prayer and devotion, they may be divided into three broad categories:

1. Sacred actions—signing the cross, genuflecting.
2. Blessings—prayers and rituals, sprinkling or signing with holy water, laying on of hands, incensing.
3. Objects that aid us in worship and devotion—candles, blessed ashes and palms, Bibles, crucifixes, medals, statues, religious art.

The existence and popularity of sacramentals testify to the diversity of prayer in the Church and that prayer can involve all our senses and go beyond words.

Pray a decade of the rosary, part of the Liturgy of the Hours, or the Angelus as a group. Then capture your reaction(s) in your journal:

How did God speak to you in this prayer?

Would you like to pray this again or try a different prayer next session?

Journey of Faith for Adults: Inquiry, Q8 (826252).
Imprimi Potest: Stephen T. Rehrauer, CSsR, Provincial, Denver Province, the Redemptorists
Imprimatur: "In accordance with CIC 827, permission to publish has been granted on March 7, 2016, by the Most Reverend Edward M. Rice, Auxiliary Bishop, Archdiocese of St. Louis. Permission to publish is an indication that nothing contrary to Church teaching is contained in this work. It does not imply any endorsement of the opinions expressed in the publication; nor is any liability assumed by this permission."

Contributing writer: Fr. Gary Ziuraitis. Excerpts from *Modern Catholic Dictionary* by Fr. John A. Hardon, SJ © 2000 Eternal Life Publications. *Embracing the Icon of Love* by Br. Daniel Korn, CSsR, © 2015 Liguori Publications. Editors of 2016 *Journey of Faith:* Denise Bossert, Julia DiSalvo, and Joan McKamey. Design: Lorena Mitre Jimenez. Images: Shutterstock.

Compliant with *The Roman Missal, Third Edition*.
Printed in the United States of America. 20 19 18 17 16 / 5 4 3 2 1. Third Edition.

Journaling

Note which prayer your group selects and ask participants the lesson's question, "Would you like to pray this again or try a different prayer next session?" Invite them to share their thoughts before the closing prayer or at the next session.

Closing Prayer

Solicit any special intentions, then close with a prayer from the lesson, perhaps one decade of the rosary if not chosen for journaling. If participants received a rosary, have them use it now.

Looking Ahead

Lesson *Q9 The Mass* explains the meaning of and various parts within the Church's highest and most perfect prayer. Encourage them to attend Mass this week and to reflect on their experience, perhaps in their journal, especially in terms of how it compares with their expectations and past prayer practices.

Q9: The Mass

Catechism: 1341–1405

Objectives

Participants will…

- recall the two parts and some major actions/events in the order of the Mass, including their respective functions and importance.
- identify the liturgy as the re-presentation of the paschal mystery—Christ's redeeming sacrifice—and a sign of the Church's unity.
- begin to recognize the reality of the Real Presence in the Eucharist.

Leader Meditation

Luke 22:14–20

Reflect on the meaning the Mass has for you. Make a renewed effort to remain focused on the liturgy next Sunday and to receive the Body and Blood with unwavering affirmation that you are receiving the Real Presence. When you kneel after Communion, ask our Lord to strengthen you and fill you with the Spirit as you lead others to the sacramental life of the Church.

Related *Catholic Updates*

- "A Walk Through the Mass" (C1109A)
- "Nine Reasons for Going to Mass: Thanksgiving Every Sunday" (C1211A)
- "The *Lectionary*: Heart of the Bible" (C9010A)

Leader Preparation

- Read the lesson, this lesson plan, the Scripture passage, and the *Catechism* sections.
- Be familiar with the many terms in this lesson: Eucharist, Mass, liturgy, introductory rites, penitential act, Gloria, Liturgy of the Word, psalm, Alleluia, homily, *Lectionary*, petitions (Universal Prayer), Liturgy of the Eucharist, offertory, consecration, Real Presence. Definitions can be found in this guide's glossary, with additional information and details available in *The Roman Missal*.
- Ask your pastor or liturgical director if the RCIA group can provide the intercessions for Mass one Sunday. If so, use the lesson's activity as a foundational draft and encourage all participants and sponsors to attend.
- Gather Mass and Mass-reading resources: a copy of *The Roman Missal, Lectionary*, among others.
- If possible, gather copies of a simple spiritual-communion prayer for distribution.

Welcome

Greet everyone as they enter with a sign of peace and the words, "Peace be with you." Explain that this gesture of reconciliation and unity is made at every Mass. Inquire about their preferred prayers and open the session with one if desired. Begin promptly.

Opening Scripture

Luke 22:14–20

Light the candle and read the passage aloud. Have participants imagine they are gathered around a table with Jesus and hearing these words directly from his mouth. Ask them to picture Jesus sharing the bread and the wine with them as they celebrate their love and friendship. Allow for a moment of silence or reread key verses and phrases. Then ask, "How do you give thanks to God? What do you 'eagerly desire' in your relationship with Christ and the Church?"

"It was above all on 'the first day of the week,' Sunday, the day of Jesus' resurrection, that the Christians met 'to break bread.' …Today we encounter [the celebration of the Eucharist] everywhere in the Church with the same fundamental structure. It remains the center of the Church's life." CCC 1343

Q9 INQUIRY

In Short:

- The Mass has two main parts.
- The Mass makes present Christ's dying and rising.
- Jesus is truly present in the Eucharist.

"Then [Jesus] took the bread, said the blessing, broke it, and gave it to them, saying, 'This is my body, which will be given for you; do this in memory of me.' And likewise the cup after they had eaten, saying, 'This cup is the new covenant in my blood, which will be shed for you.'"

Luke 22:19–20

The Mass

The Mass is so important to Catholics that we participate in it every Sunday or Saturday evening. Many Catholics also attend Mass on weekdays.

Mass has been important enough over the centuries that people have died defending and exercising their religious freedom to participate in the Mass. In some places still today, Catholic priests offer the Mass in secret.

- *What regular activities do you consider essential in your life? Why?*

Why Is the Mass So Important?

At Mass, Catholics remember what Jesus did at the Last Supper. Jesus' words, "Do this in memory of me" have been obeyed without interruption for more than 2,000 years. Every time Catholics gather for Mass, we know we're there to do what Jesus commanded. And we believe that Jesus is made present to us.

Also known as the sacrament or sacrifice of the **Eucharist**, the **Mass** is our most precious prayer. It is a **liturgy**, part of the public worship or "work" of the Church and is "the summit and source of our Christian life….[I]n the Eucharist is found the entire treasure of the Church—Jesus Christ" (United States Catholic Catechism for Adults, p. 228).

Let's briefly examine the principal parts of the Mass.

The Introductory Rites

The introductory rites bring the community together as one. The entrance of the priest and ministers completes the community—the people of God—in whose midst Christ is present.

As Mass begins, the priest leads us in the Sign of the Cross. We respond, "Amen." Response and participation are essential to liturgy. The prayer comes alive as each of us responds, listens, reflects, speaks, and sings.

Our awareness of God's presence reminds us that we haven't always lived as we should. We take part in a **Penitential Act**, which involves asking for and receiving God's forgiveness, perhaps with a prayer or the chant, "Lord, have mercy."

CCC 1341–1405

ADULTS

Q9

Why Is the Mass So Important?

Inform participants that lesson C5 is the *Sacrament of the Eucharist*. While ultimately the same rite, this lesson focuses on the liturgy (steps to the prayer and sacrament) while the catechumenate lesson focuses on the deep symbolism and meaning of Christ's Real Presence in the Eucharist.

Emphasize and review why the Mass is so important and valuable. The Eucharist is "the source and summit" of our faith because it is Christ himself. Even if you don't receive, you can still encounter Christ in God's word (the readings), in the assembly, and elsewhere.

Explain that as Catholics mature spiritually, the Mass evolves from an obligation to a celebration. Encourage the participants to compare how they approach social invitations with how they respond to obligations.

The Introductory Rites

Relate the Penitential Act to the Parable of the Prodigal Son if time permits (Luke 15:11–32).

The Liturgy of the Word

Review the principal parts of the Mass, making sure participants understand the purpose and meaning of the Liturgy of the Word and the Liturgy of the Eucharist.

Explain that many Catholics reflect on the Mass readings ahead of time to prepare their hearts. All the readings can be found online and in certain publications. Direct participants to the USCCB's Bible website (on usccb.org) and refer them to, or distribute, samples of other Mass-reading resources. If there's time or it's necessary, remind them that the weekday readings follow a separate two-year cycle.

Remind participants again, if necessary, that lesson E4 explores the Nicene Creed in detail.

Next comes the "Gloria," an ancient hymn of praise. The opening lines from Luke's account of Jesus' birth express our wonder at what God has done. Then the priest says, "Let us pray," and pauses for silence. Moments of silence provide space for a deeper experience of God's presence. The priest gathers or collects our prayers in a prayer called the Collect.

Why So Much Sitting, Standing, and Kneeling?

God created us with physical bodies, so we worship God with our bodies, minds, and spirits. We *stand* as a sign of reverence—when encountering Christ in the gospel, in the Eucharist, and in moments of important conversation with God. We *sit* to listen and reflect. We *kneel* to express our humility before God and our adoration of God.

"At the name of Jesus every knee should bend, of those in heaven and on earth."

Philippians 2:10

The Liturgy of the Word

The **Liturgy of the Word** is the first of two main parts of the Mass. We listen and reflect on the presence of God in the words of sacred Scripture.

1. The *First Reading* is from the Old Testament (except during the Easter season). It usually relates to the Gospel.
2. The *Responsorial* **Psalm** is a hymn of praise from the Book of Psalms in the Old Testament. The psalms were composed as song-prayers so it's usually sung or chanted with the assembled people repeating a response.
3. The *Second Reading* is from the epistles (letters) of Paul or another New Testament letter. This reading doesn't always relate to the others but exposes us to more of sacred Scripture.
4. The *Gospel Acclamation*, usually an **Alleluia**—"Praise ye the Lord"—or another acclamation during Lent, acknowledges and welcomes Christ's presence in God's word.
5. The *Gospel* reading is proclaimed by the priest or deacon and is given highest honor because it contains the words of Jesus. With a thumb, we trace a small cross on our forehead, lips, and chest and silently pray these or similar words: *May your word, O Lord, be in my thoughts, on my lips, and in my heart.*
6. The **homily** follows the Gospel. In the homily, the priest or deacon explains the Scripture proclaimed at this Mass and applies it to our lives today.

How Are the Readings Chosen?

The Sunday Mass readings are arranged so that over a three-year period almost all of the New Testament and a varied selection from the Old Testament will be proclaimed. A new cycle begins each Advent. Year A features the Gospel of Matthew; Year B, Mark; and Year C, Luke. John's Gospel is usually read during Easter, Christmas, and to fill out Year B because Mark's Gospel is short. The Mass readings are proclaimed from a book called the *Lectionary*.

7. We stand and recite the main beliefs of our faith using the words of the Nicene Creed or Apostles' Creed.
8. A deacon or lector presents our **petitions** (requests or appeals) in the **Universal Prayer**, also called the *Prayer of the Faithful* or general intercessions. After each petition we say, "Lord, hear our prayer" or a similar response.

Write Your Own Petition

Fill in the blanks to express a need to God in prayer:

For [person, group, situation] ____________________,

that [request or appeal] __________________________,

we pray to the Lord.

The Liturgy of the Eucharist

We celebrate the wondrous deeds of God in every celebration of the Liturgy of the Eucharist, the second main part of the Mass.

Preparation of the Gifts
In the **offertory** or *Presentation of the Gifts*, we express our participation by making an offering, bringing to the altar the bread and wine for the Eucharist and our monetary contributions for the needs of the Church and the poor.

The bread and wine become for us the Body and Blood of Christ. God, who is never outdone in generosity, returns to us more than we could ever give.

- *What can you offer God this week? How can your life become a living offering? (Mark 12:33; Ephesians 5:1–2)*

The Eucharistic Prayer

This prayer is the center and highest point of the Mass. It's spoken by the priest but is the prayer of the entire community.

1. *Acclamation of Praise.* All the faithful in heaven and on earth join in a song or chant of praise. The words of the *Sanctus* (Holy, Holy) come from Isaiah 6:3: "Holy, holy, holy is the LORD of hosts! All the earth is filled with his glory!" and Matthew 21:9: "Blessed is he who comes in the name of the Lord; hosanna in the highest."
2. *Calling Upon God to Send the Spirit.* The priest asks God to send the Holy Spirit to achieve a twofold conversion: changing the bread and wine into the Body and Blood of Christ and conforming us into the image of Christ.
3. *Institution Narrative and Consecration.* The priest recounts the Last Supper: how Jesus took the bread, blessed it, gave thanks, and said, "Take and eat; this is my body." Then he took a cup, gave thanks, and gave it to them, saying, "Drink from it, all of you, for this is my blood of the covenant, which will be shed on behalf of many for the forgiveness of sins" (Matthew 26:26–28).

   In this moment of **consecration**, "the power of the words and the action of Christ, and the power of the Holy Spirit, make sacramentally present, under the species of bread and wine, Christ's Body and Blood, his sacrifice offered on the cross for all" (*CCC* 1353). We call this the **Real Presence** of Christ in the Eucharist.
4. *Memorial Acclamation.* The people proclaim "the mystery of faith"—that Jesus died for our sins, rose from death, and will return in glory.
5. *Remembering.* God's saving actions, accomplished in Christ, are remembered, not as past events but as events that continue to accomplish their effects here and now. Remembering isn't just a recalling of the past; it's making the past present in our midst. This bringing of the past into the present is what Jesus meant when he said, "Do this in memory of me."

Write Your Own Petition

Complete this activity during the session. Have participants take turns reading their petitions aloud during the Closing Prayer.

The Liturgy of the Eucharist

Explain that the Sign of Peace prayer (perhaps modeled in your Welcome) reflects Jesus' first words after the resurrection: "Peace be with you." It is rooted in his admonition from the Sermon on the Mount: "If you bring your gift to the altar, and there recall that your brother has anything against you, leave your gift [and] go first and be reconciled with your brother..." (Matthew 5:23–24). Reaching out to one another admits our interdependence and helps to effect the unity of the Mass.

Instruct participants in basic Mass decorum. If they are attending regularly and not dismissed after the Liturgy of the Word, explain that they may remain in their pew and pray during communion or process through the line to receive a blessing from the minister (*not* to receive the Eucharist). If the latter, model the proper position which indicates this intention (arms crossed over the chest).

Discuss how the Mass (Eucharist) builds relationships between God and his people and among the people themselves. Invite sponsors and team members to share experiences of growth and community emerging from the Mass.

6. *Offering.* The offering of Jesus is accompanied with prayers of intercession for the entire Church, living and dead. The priest raises the bread and chalice—a gesture suggestive of offering. It's no longer Jesus alone who is offered to the Father; it's now Jesus *with* the Church.

7. *Great Amen.* An enthusiastic "Amen" places the seal of the community's approval on all that's been said and done in the Eucharistic Prayer.

The Communion Rite

1. *The Lord's Prayer.* This prayer reminds us that God is our Father and that we depend on him for everything.

2. *The Sign of Peace.* We exchange a sign of unity and communion with one another and with God.

3. *Communion.* Following the Lamb of God prayer asking for God's mercy, we receive the Body and Blood of the Lord in holy Communion. We, though many, become one body in Christ. Each of us is empowered to share in the life and work of Christ, to bring him to all we meet.

The Concluding Rites

Following a blessing, the priest or deacon commissions those assembled to live out the challenges of the Gospel, bringing Christ to the world and also discovering him there.

- *What is your life's purpose? What might your mission be as Christ's disciple?*

Compare the Mass to the family table, where a family comes together to nourish and embrace each member as part of the family unit.

- *What, including food, is brought to the table?*
- *How does each person contribute and participate?*

Journey of Faith for Adults: Inquiry, Q9 (826252)
Imprimi Potest: Stephen T. Rehrauer, CSsR, Provincial, Denver Province, the Redemptorists.
Imprimatur: "In accordance with CIC 827, permission to publish has been granted on March 7, 2016, by the Most Reverend Edward M. Rice, Auxiliary Bishop, Archdiocese of St. Louis. Permission to publish is an indication that nothing contrary to Church teaching is contained in this work. It does not imply any endorsement of the opinions expressed in the publication, nor is any liability assumed by this permission."

Contributing writers: Fr. Robert Riecheck, CSsR, Br. Daniel Korn, CSsR, Fr. James Ryan, CSsR, Fr. Oscar Lukefahr, CM; William H. Shannon. Editors of 2016 edition: Denise Bossert, Julia DiSalvo, and Joan McKamey. Design: Lorena Mitre Jimenez. Images: Shutterstock.

Printed in the United States of America. 20 19 18 17 16 / 5 4 3 2 1. Third Edition.

Journaling

Help participants make these connections and share their responses during the session. If time is used in discussion, the writing may take place at home.

Closing Prayer

Review or teach the intercessory formula: concluding each petition with "We pray to the Lord" so the group can respond, "Lord, hear our prayer." After each participant reads his or her petition, close with a recitation of the Lord's Prayer, which is prayed at every Mass.

Looking Ahead

Lesson *Q10 The Church Year* discusses the Mass in the context of the liturgical calendar, which progresses through the life of Christ and the Church. Invite participants to Mass again, this time preparing them to note the liturgical feast and any meaningful readings or symbols.

Q10: The Church Year

Catechism: 524–25, 1095, 1163–73, 1194–95

Objectives

Participants will…

- name the seasons of the Church year in order and their respective colors, symbols, and themes.
- identify the cyclical nature of the liturgical calendar and some related feasts, particularly holy days.
- recognize how the order of readings and feasts results in a full and meaningful proclamation of Scripture and integration of the life of the Church into the life, death, and resurrection of Christ.

Leader Meditation

Ecclesiastes 3:1; Mark 13:28–29

Reflect on the liturgical calendar and what its structure offers for the expression of our faith, the sense of rhythm and rightness it brings to Church life, and the channel or passageway it provides to all the faithful for entering into the paschal mystery.

Related *Catholic Update*

"The Liturgical Year: How Christians Celebrate Time" (C9511A)

Leader Preparation

- Read the lesson, this lesson plan, the opening Scripture, and the *Catechism* sections.
- Be familiar with the many terms in this lesson: Annunciation, Church Year/liturgical year, Advent, Christmas, Ordinary Time, Lent, Holy Week, Palm Sunday, penitence, Triduum, paschal mystery, Easter, feast (day), holy day of obligation, ascension, assumption (of Mary), immaculate conception, Nativity. Definitions can be found in this guide's glossary.
- Gather copies of a current liturgical chart or calendar for participants and sponsors. Some parishes, organizations, and groups provide these for free as Advent approaches, and others can be purchased year-round. If Advent is near, also consider providing a Jesse tree resource for your RCIA families.

Welcome

Greet the members of the group as they gather. Check for supplies and immediate needs. Solicit questions or comments about the previous session and/or share new information and findings. Begin promptly.

Opening Scriptures

Ecclesiastes 3:1; Mark 13:28–29

Light the candle and read the passages aloud. Allow for a moment of silence, and then invite participants to share examples of routines and habits in their work or family life that provide order and reflect priorities and values. Ask, "How does setting aside time for a task or relationship give it meaning and value?" Explain that the Church year's purpose is the same.

> "Holy Mother Church believes that she should celebrate the saving work of her divine Spouse in a sacred commemoration on certain days throughout the course of the year. Once each week, on the day which she has called the Lord's Day, she keeps the memory of the Lord's resurrection….In the course of the year, moreover, she unfolds the whole mystery of Christ."
>
> CCC 1163

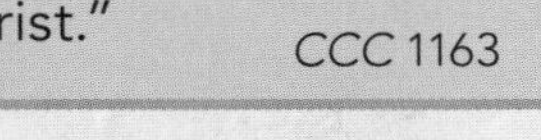

Q10

INQUIRY

In Short:

- With Sundays at its center, the Church year follows a pattern of seasons.
- The Church calendar includes feasts, holy days, and saints' days.
- Colors, symbols, and themes have deep meanings.

The Church Year

Christians long to retrace the steps of Jesus and walk with him through his life on earth. The Gospel writers did it. Anyone who has made a pilgrimage to the Holy Land has done it. As we hear the stories and follow the path year after year, we discover new truths and understand more deeply.

The fulfillment of our salvation through Jesus begins with the annunciation—Mary's consent to the archangel Gabriel's announcement that she had been chosen by God to be the Mother of his Son (Luke 1:26–38). The story unfolds as the magi arrive with gifts and the Holy Family flees to Egypt (Matthew 2). We observe the presentation of Jesus in the Temple (Luke 2:22–38) and search with Mary and Joseph for their lost Child some years later (2:41–50).

We see Jesus at his baptism in the Jordan, at his first miracle at a wedding in Cana, and at the Sea of Galilee as he calls his first disciples. We see him in Jerusalem and walk with him as he carries his cross. We see the tomb where he was laid and where death was defeated by his resurrection. We watch him ascend to heaven and wait with Mary and the apostles for the coming of the Holy Spirit.

The Church, like the Gospel writers, retells the story in time. Over the course of a year, the Church celebrates all these events, beginning with Christ's Incarnation and birth and ending with his Second Coming.

> *"In the course of the year...[the Church] unfolds the whole mystery of Christ."*
>
> CCC 1163

- *What part(s) of Jesus' story do you want to know more about?*
- *How can Jesus' story speak to and guide your own story?*

Liturgical Seasons

Like our natural year, the **Church year** follows a pattern of seasons. Also called the **liturgical year**, the Church year celebrates and relives the great events of our salvation. Each year follows a pattern, and our prayers and readings for Mass guide us in our celebrations.

Advent

During **Advent**, we share in the Israelites' long wait for the Messiah and enter into expectation and anticipation for the coming of our Savior. The season begins on the fourth Sunday before Christmas.

This time is one of joyful anticipation, of waiting in hope with Mary for the birth of our Lord.

CCC 524–25, 1095, 1163–73, 1194–95

ADULTS

Q10

The Church Year

Remind participants that, like a family, the Church gathers in times of joy and sorrow, in times of accomplishment, blessing, remembrance, loss, and crisis.

Liturgical Seasons

Review the order of liturgical seasons and their respective events, colors, symbols, and themes. Discuss how these details bring life and an added dimension to the ever-unfolding celebration of the events in the life of Christ and the Church.

Display or distribute a Jesse tree, especially if Advent is approaching. Explain the various symbols and biblical figures and their role in salvation history.

Discuss the symbols and themes of Holy Week, the Triduum, and Pentecost, which are not explicit in the lesson, if there's time.

Review the date for Easter, reminding participants they will enter the Church on the night before.

Catholics are encouraged to "keep Advent"—to avoid rushing into Christmas. In addition to preparing our hearts for the celebration of Christ's birth, we also prepare our hearts for Jesus' Second Coming and the fullness of the kingdom. An important way we prepare is by examining our lives and celebrating the sacrament of penance and reconciliation.

Liturgical color: violet for royalty, humility, and hope

Traditions: Advent wreaths and calendars that help families count down to Christmas are common traditions. An Advent wreath is made of evergreen and holds four candles: three purple (violet) and one pink (rose). Each of the four Sundays of Advent is marked by the lighting of a candle. The candle for the third Sunday is pink as a sign of our joy that Christmas is near.

Christmas

The **Christmas** season marks the birth of Jesus. It lasts from Christmas Day until the feast of the Baptism of the Lord in early January. There are many special celebrations during this season.

Liturgical color: white for light, innocence, and joy

Traditions: Many Catholics intentionally leave up the Christmas tree, continue to display the Nativity scene, and joyfully sing Christmas carols and hymns long after the secular world sets them aside.

Ordinary Time

Ordinary Time follows the Christmas season for several weeks. It's a time for reflecting on the mystery of Christ's life and growing as a Church.

Liturgical color: green for growth and eternal life

Lent

Lent is a penitential season that lasts forty days, beginning on Ash Wednesday and ending at the start of the Easter Triduum. During Lent, Catholics prepare themselves for the holiest days of the year. In anticipation of the renewal of their baptismal promises and the reception of new members into the Church, Catholics pray, fast, give alms, and celebrate the sacrament of penance. The final week, also called **Holy Week**, begins with **Palm Sunday**, which recounts Jesus' entry into Jerusalem (Matthew 21:1–9) and his suffering and death that follow.

Liturgical color: violet for **penitence**: sorrow and repentance for one's sins

Triduum

The **Triduum**, Latin for "three days," begins with the Mass of the Lord's Supper on Holy Thursday evening and continues through Good Friday and Holy Saturday until the evening of Easter Sunday. "Though chronologically three days, they are liturgically one day unfolding for us the unity of Christ's paschal mystery. The single celebration of the Triduum marks the end of the Lenten season, and leads to the Mass of the Resurrection of the Lord at the Easter Vigil" (U.S. Conference of Catholic Bishops).

Liturgical colors: Holy Thursday: white
Good Friday: red
Holy Saturday and Easter Sunday: white

TRIDUUM
LENT
MARCH
ORDINARY TIME
FEBRUARY
JANUARY
ADVENT CHRISTMAS TIME
DECEMBER
NOVEMBER

Th
Liturg
Caler

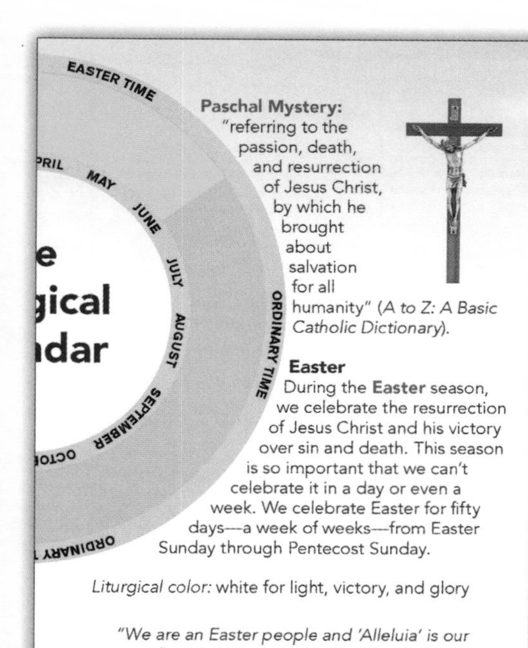

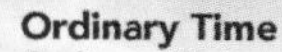

Paschal Mystery: "referring to the passion, death, and resurrection of Jesus Christ, by which he brought about salvation for all humanity" (*A to Z: A Basic Catholic Dictionary*).

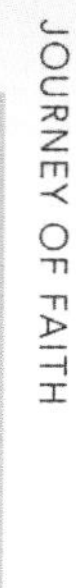

Easter

During the **Easter** season, we celebrate the resurrection of Jesus Christ and his victory over sin and death. This season is so important that we can't celebrate it in a day or even a week. We celebrate Easter for fifty days—a week of weeks—from Easter Sunday through Pentecost Sunday.

Liturgical color: white for light, victory, and glory

> *"We are an Easter people and 'Alleluia' is our song."*
>
> *Attributed to St. Augustine*

Since Jesus died during the Jewish Passover festival, the date of Easter is calculated accordingly. At the Council of Nicaea (AD 325), it was decided that Easter, the Christian Passover, should be celebrated on the Sunday after the first full moon following the first day of spring. This means Easter doesn't occur on the same date each year—unlike Christmas, which always falls on December 25.

- *What is the date for next Easter? How might its celebration be more meaningful to you?*

?

Ordinary Time

Ordinary Time returns following the Easter season and ends the last Sunday before Advent: the feast of Christ the King. Ordinary Time is a time for reflecting on the mystery of Christ's life and growing as a Church.

Liturgical color: green for growth and eternal life

Rhyme and Reason

Our lives follow rhythms similar to the cycle of the Church year. Whether these rhythms are in step or not, the Church guides us through the cycle and seasons of the life, death, and resurrection of Jesus.

On our high days—times of discovery, accomplishment, fulfillment, commitment, and authenticity—the Church shows us how to celebrate these gifts with joy.

In times of disappointment, struggle, weakness, failure, and loss, the Church reminds us that light follows darkness, spring follows winter, and Easter follows Good Friday.

In times of coming and going, falling down and getting back up, learning to love and asking for forgiveness, the Church reminds us of God's faithful and enduring presence.

As we move through the liturgical year, with its different themes and postures of the heart, we support and celebrate the times of Advent waiting and Christmas celebrations, the sorrows of Good Friday and Easter joys of new life and community. The Church year helps us connect our own stories with the story of God, helping us find greater meaning in every part of life.

The Importance of Sunday

Explain briefly the concept of sabbath if participants aren't familiar with the term or Jewish tradition.

Holy Days of Obligation

Review the holy days of obligation and what is required of Catholics on such days. While RCIA participants are not yet bound by this precept (*CCC* 2043), encourage them to consider participating or celebrating in a smaller way as an act of love and solidarity.

Encourage participants to mark special feasts and celebrate the saints within their own homes. Pick a saint and give examples of how they might make his or her feast particularly engaging and meaningful—preparing a culturally- or historically-themed meal or activity, reading a short biography of or writing from the saint, etc.

Explain the distinction and order among feasts, solemnities, and memorials, if there's time. This can be illustrated easily using examples from a liturgical calendar. Note the connection between various feasts—for instance, how the feast of the Annunciation (March 25) is celebrated nine months before Christmas.

The Importance of Sunday

> *"The Lord's day, the day of Resurrection, the day of Christians, is our day. It is called the Lord's day because on it the Lord rose victorious to the Father. If pagans call it the 'day of the sun,' we willingly agree, for today the light of the world is raised, today is revealed the sun of justice with healing in his rays."*
>
> St. Jerome, *In die dominica paschae homilia, CCL* 78, 550

Sunday, the "Lord's day," is central to our liturgical life. Our observance begins on the Saturday evening before, and all Catholics are obligated to participate in Mass every weekend. There, "the Lord's Supper is its center, for there the whole community of the faithful encounters the risen Lord who invites them to his banquet" (*CCC* 1166).

The Church also encourages us to treat Sunday as a day of rest, recreation, and family time as a way of keeping the Third Commandment: "Remember the sabbath day—keep it holy. Six days you may labor and do all your work, but the seventh day is a sabbath of the LORD your God" (Exodus 20:8–10).

- *How do you spend Sundays?*
- *How can you "keep it holy?"*

Holy Days of Obligation

The Church year is full of **feast days** celebrating Jesus, Mary, and the saints. In the United States, six of these are **holy days of obligation.** Like Sundays, Catholics make these days holy by attending Mass and refraining from unnecessary work:

- Mary, the Holy Mother of God—January 1
- The **Ascension** of the Lord—forty days after Easter or the following Sunday
- The **Assumption of Mary**—August 15
- All Saints' Day—November 1
- The **Immaculate Conception** of Mary—December 8
- The **Nativity** of the Lord (Christmas)—December 25

Reflect on your typical day, week, or year. What routines or traditions do you have? When is your next vacation, family celebration, or home improvement? Mark the following:

- Times of high energy or positive emotion
- Times of study or preparation
- Times of calm, quiet, or relaxation
- Fixed or set times
- Flexible or movable times
- Times with community

Pray to God and invite him to be part of all the "times" of your life.

Journey of Faith for Adults: Inquiry, Q10 (826252)
Imprimi Potest: Stephen T. Rehrauer, CSsR, Provincial, Denver Province, the Redemptorists.
Imprimatur: "In accordance with CIC 827, permission to publish has been granted on March 7, 2016, by the Most Reverend Edward M. Rice, Auxiliary Bishop, Archdiocese of St. Louis. Permission to publish is an indication that nothing contrary to Church teaching is contained in this work. It does not imply any endorsement of the opinions expressed in the publication, nor is any liability assumed by this permission."

Printed in the United States of America. 20 19 18 17 16 / 5 4 3 2 1. Third Edition.

Journaling

Provide time during the session to complete, or at least begin, this activity. Give participants freedom and artistic license to design their schedule, calendar, or chart however it best expresses their experience. If there's time, go around the room sharing one another's special times.

Closing Prayer

Request petitions from the group, and then thank God for the gift of the Church year (liturgical calendar), which unites the Church and deepens our faith, just as family gatherings and traditions become a bond among the members. Consider reciting a seasonal prayer, liturgical prayer, or preface from *The Roman Missal* or the Liturgy of the Hours.

Looking Ahead

Lesson *Q11 Places in a Catholic Church*, describes and discusses the objects and symbols people encounter within a physical church building, chapel, or shrine. Before or after Mass this week, have participants walk or at least look around the parish church, noticing the many areas, objects, symbols, and colors within a single place.

Q11: Places in a Catholic Church

Catechism: 1179–86, 1192, 1198–99

Objectives

Participants will…

- recall places and objects within a typical parish church and why they're significant or what they're used for.
- recognize the church as a place for public and private prayer.
- realize when we gather together in church Christ is with us.

Leader Meditation

Psalm 84

Take your Bible to church and kneel silently before the Lord. Pray for the wisdom and insight to instruct the participants. Be aware of the sacred elements in the church and meditate on the many ways these items have touched your life.

Related *Catholic Update*

"A Tour of a Catholic Church" (C9103A)

Leader Preparation

- Read the lesson, this lesson plan, the opening Scripture, and the *Catechism* sections.
- Be familiar with the many terms in this lesson: parish, sanctuary, altar, *The Roman Missal* (formerly sacramentary), ambo, lectern, crucifix, tabernacle, sanctuary lamp, narthex/gathering space (vestibule), holy water (font), baptismal font, Easter (paschal) candle, Stations (Way) of the Cross, reconciliation chapel (confessional), sacristy, vestments, alb, cincture, chasuble, dalmatic, stole, rectory, convent, monastery, cloister, friary, abbey, (arch)diocese, (arch)bishop, deanery, chancery, cathedral, basilica, Vatican, pilgrimage, shrine. Definitions can be found in this guide's glossary.
- Schedule a tour of the church, sacristy, chapel, or a local shrine or prayer center. Whether or not this replaces the formal session, provide participants with quiet time for prayer in a sacred or holy place. If a group tour isn't available, strongly encourage sponsors to accompany their inquirer or candidate in a private visit to the church.
- Ask the pastor or deacon to assist you in displaying (and perhaps pronouncing) the various vestments to the participants. If he isn't available, simply borrowing a few items will suffice. If not included in the tour, also borrow a few liturgical objects or sacred vessels from the sacristry.
- Research the histories and missions of your parish and diocese. Consider gathering a list of names, websites, and relevant contact information for participants and sponsors.
- Remind team members and sponsors (and yourself) to bring personal photos or mementos from religious trips to this session.

Welcome

Welcome participants and sponsors as they arrive. Solicit questions or comments about the previous session and begin promptly.

Opening Scripture

Psalm 84

Light the candle and read the psalm aloud. If in church, have it proclaimed or sung by a lector or cantor at the ambo. Explain how the church building (or this location) is special or unique from any other place. Emphasize that it is God's "dwelling place," holy and set apart. Point out your favorite features, spaces, or items. Invite participants to react to or compare its beauty to other locations.

> "In its earthly state the Church needs places where the community can gather together. Our visible churches, holy places, are images of the holy city, the heavenly Jerusalem toward which we are making our way on pilgrimage." CCC 1198

In Short:

- Catholics use their parish church for public worship and personal prayer.
- Every place and object in a church building has special significance.
- When we gather in church, Christ is in our midst.

- *Describe a place that's sacred or holy to you.*
- *To what or to whom is your local parish dedicated? How does the parish share that event or person's story?*

Places in a Catholic Church

Where do you feel a strong presence of God? Maybe you think of a forest, a mountain, or the ocean. Perhaps a place where you felt safe and loved as a child comes to mind. God is everywhere, but certain places help us feel his presence more profoundly. Catholics encounter God in many places. In fact, you've likely already visited a place Catholics believe "exists solely for the good of souls" (Pope Paul VI, *Christus Dominus*, 31).

That place is the local **parish**. The term parish can refer to the community and to the buildings used by the community, just as the term church can refer to the faith community and to the building where Catholics gather to pray.

Most parishes have territorial boundaries and serve the people of the local area. Some parishes aren't territorial but serve specific groups with particular nationalities, languages, or rites. A parish may be named to honor a person of the Trinity, a saint, or a significant event in the life of Jesus or Mary.

Although each church is unique, we expect to find certain things in all of them. The following will help you understand some key symbols and objects you'll find in a Catholic church building.

The Sanctuary: Front and Center

The **sanctuary** (1) is the main area of focus for liturgical ceremonies. In this area, you'll find the main **altar** (2) or Lord's table, which is the focus of the Liturgy of the Eucharist. During the Eucharistic Prayer, the offerings of bread and wine brought to this altar become the Body and Blood of Christ. At the altar, the priest reads from the ***Roman Missal*** (3), the book of prayers used at Mass. Candles adorn the altar to symbolize Christ's presence and light.

Often to one side of the altar is the **ambo** (4). You'll find the Lectionary, the book of Mass readings, here. What happens here is the focus of the Liturgy of the Word. Nonscriptural reading and song leading may occur at a secondary **lectern** (5).

A cross or **crucifix** (6)—a cross containing the image of Christ's body—reminds us of his suffering and death. You'll find one placed either on or near the altar. It may be used in procession at the beginning and end of Mass.

ADULTS

CCC 1179–86, 1192, 1198–99

Places in a Catholic Church

Invite participants to share and describe their "holy places" in response to the lesson's first question. Assure them that prayer is good at any time and in any place—as long as it's directed to the one, true God.

Ask, "Why is the church a special place to pray?" Discuss how it provides a quiet and peaceful setting and facilitates worship and adoration. Be sure to mention the significance of the Eucharist, altar, tabernacle, and baptismal font (holy water).

Allow participants, then sponsors, to share any knowledge of the parish's patronage and history, then provide details or distribute information that connects them further to their parish and diocese.

The Sanctuary: Front and Center

Locate and talk about the places and symbols in your church (location) as they are described. If on a tour, this will require the group to move about. Once you finish, transition to the journaling, if there's time.

Instruct participants on proper reverence and etiquette when approaching the sanctuary. The tabernacle's location may depend on the architecture and date of your church's construction.

Other Places in Church

If it is possible to tour your church, invite all participants to bless themselves with the water and Sign of the Cross at the holy water or baptismal font. *There are many things they cannot do, but crossing themselves with holy water is possible whenever they enter and exit church (except during the Triduum).* In some (particularly older) churches, the baptismal font is fixed in a rear room or area called the *baptistry*.

Emphasize that the Stations of the Cross are more than decoration or religious artwork. They are used for prayer and devotion and often blessed as sacramental objects. Tell participants that the group will practice the stations during Lent (in lesson E5). If there's time, walk through each station and mention the event and its connection to Scripture.

JOURNEY OF FAITH INQUIRY

The **tabernacle** (7) is a special receptacle in which the eucharistic bread is reserved for the purpose of bringing Communion to the sick and for private devotion. The **sanctuary lamp** (8), often red in color, houses a candle that continuously burns near the tabernacle to remind us of Jesus' presence there. The tabernacle may be in the main space of the church or in a separate room or space nearby.

Do Catholics Worship Images?

The crucifix is a symbol that reminds us of the salvation won through Christ's death and resurrection. Images of Christ remind us of St. Paul's mandate to "proclaim Christ crucified" (1 Corinthians 1:23). Catholics don't worship the images of Jesus or the saints found in Catholic churches and homes. God alone is worthy of our worship. These images in statues, stained-glass windows, paintings, and mosaics are just visible representations of spiritual realities. Through them, we grow in appreciation for and union with what they represent—the living and divine person of Christ and the saints in heaven.

Things and places in the Catholic chu

1. Sanctuary 2. Altar 3. *Roman Missal* 4. Ambo 5. Le
9. Holy water 10. Baptismal font 11. Easter (paschal) c

Other Places in Church

1. Most parishes have a **narthex** or **gathering space** that divides the main entrance from the nave, the people's worship area. The narthex may feature pamphlet racks or bulletin boards and be used for fellowship before and after Mass. It also functions as a starting place for processions, certain rites, and to transition between the liturgy and everyday life.
2. When you walk into church, you'll see a small bowl of water. This is a font containing **holy water** (9) that has been blessed by a priest to be used as a reminder of baptism. The faithful dip the tips of their fingers into the water and make the Sign of the Cross as they enter and leave the church.
3. The **baptismal font** (10) is a large, raised vessel or basin in which holy water is contained for baptisms. It's found in a prominent place, either near the entrance of the church or in the sanctuary. In churches where baptism by immersion is performed, the font may be a larger pool. When placed near the main entrance, a baptismal font may also serve as the holy water font.
4. The **Easter** (or **paschal**) **candle** (11) is a large, ornamented candle symbolic of the risen Christ and often positioned near the altar, lectern, or baptismal font. During the Easter season, it burns at every liturgy. It's also placed next to the casket during funerals as a sign of our hope in the resurrection and of our faith that Christ will receive the departed into the fullness of his kingdom.
5. The **Stations of the Cross** (12) (also **Way of the Cross**) are fourteen crosses or images representing or depicting the steps Jesus took to his death. They are usually located along the inside walls of the church. Catholics use them to meditate on Christ's suffering.
6. The **reconciliation chapel**, sometimes called the confessional or reconciliation room, is a private space where a person celebrates the sacrament of penance and reconciliation. Most of these provide for confessions to be made anonymously (behind a screen) or face to face with the priest.

- *How does it feel to know that your baptismal or confirmation candle will be lit by the Easter candle, spiritually joining you to Christ?*

ctern 6. Crucifix 7. Tabernacle 8. Sanctuary lamp
andle 12. Stations of the Cross 13. Sacristy

"I am the light of the world. Whoever follows me will not walk in darkness, but will have the light of life."

John 8:12

Clerical Vestments

The **sacristy** (13) is the room where the priest and ministers prepare for liturgical services and put on their religious garments called **vestments.** The main vestments worn at Mass are:

1. An **alb**: a long, white garment symbolic of the purity one should have when approaching God. Priests, deacons, and altar servers wear albs.
2. A **cincture**: a belt or cord, often white, worn around the waist over the alb.
3. A **chasuble**: the outermost garment worn by the priest during Mass. The color of the chasuble matches the liturgical season or feast. Deacons may wear a similar but shorter garment called a **dalmatic**.
4. A **stole**: a narrow, fabric band that's worn around the neck by priests and bishops. A deacon wears a stole over his left shoulder like a sash.

- *How does what you wear to church symbolize the way you feel about God?*

Also on the Parish Campus

Outside of church, parish activities may be held in a gym, cafeteria, hall, or parish center. The **rectory** is where the priest or priests reside. If a religious institute is associated with your parish or nearby, its members may live in a communal home. These homes go by various names: **convent**, **monastery**, **cloister**, **friary**, or **abbey**.

Types of Churches

A **diocese** is a geographical area entrusted to the pastoral care of a **bishop**. Examples of dioceses in the United States are Albany and Baton Rouge. A large or significant diocese is called an **archdiocese**, which is led by an **archbishop**. Three U.S. archdioceses are St. Louis, Chicago, and Los Angeles. A diocese or archdiocese may be subdivided into **deaneries** consisting of several parishes, and all are divided into parishes. The (arch) bishop's offices and programs are centralized in the **chancery**, sometimes called the diocesan curia or Catholic Center.

A **cathedral** is the (arch)bishop's official parish church. The Latin word cathedra means "chair," which is the symbol of the bishop's leadership. The pope's cathedral is the Basilica of St. John Lateran. A **basilica** is a church designated as a place of special historical or architectural (artistic) importance. As the traditional "home parish" of the pope, the Lateran Basilica is considered more important than any other church, even St. Peter's in Vatican City.

The **Vatican** is the worldwide administrative headquarters of the Catholic Church and the pope's official residence.

- *In what (arch)diocese is your parish located? What is the name and location of the cathedral?*

Also on the Parish Campus

Walk the parish grounds to acquaint participants with the rectory, parish center, convent, or any other building central to the life of the parish, if weather and time allow.

Other Religious Places

Invite sponsors and team members to share personal experiences (and even photos) of pilgrimages or religious trips they've taken. Mention other well-known sites or Catholic destinations in your area.

JOURNEY OF FAITH INQUIRY

Other Religious Places

In Old Testament times, the Israelites went on pilgrimage—a journey to a sacred place—to the Temple in Jerusalem. Here they could worship, pray, and encounter God in a deeper way. The Holy Land is another popular destination for both Jews and Christians today. Pilgrims sail on the Sea of Galilee and visit places where Jesus and the apostles lived, taught, healed, and nurtured the growth of early Christian communities.

Catholics also visit **shrines**. A shrine may be where a holy object—statue, image, or relic—is housed. It may also be the location of a saint's life or burial, a miracle, or an appearance of the Blessed Virgin Mary.

- *If you could make a pilgrimage to anywhere in the world, where would it be? Why?*

Think of all the Catholic symbols, objects, and places you know so far. Pick one that represents your journey of faith. Explain your choice in your prayer journal.

***Journey of Faith for Adults: Inquiry*, Q11 (826252)**
Imprimi Potest: Stephen T. Rehrauer, CSsR, Provincial, Denver Province, the Redemptorists.
Imprimatur: "In accordance with CIC 827, permission to publish has been granted on March 7, 2016, by the Most Reverend Edward M. Rice, Auxiliary Bishop, Archdiocese of St. Louis. Permission to publish is an indication that nothing contrary to Church teaching is contained in this work. It does not imply any endorsement of the opinions expressed in the publication, nor is any liability assumed by this permission."

Contributing writers: Fr. Gary Ziuraitis, CSsR; Fr. Daniel L. Lowery, CSsR; Terry Matz. Editors of 2016 edition: Denise Bossert, Julia DiSalvo, and Joan McKamey. Design: Lorena Mitre Jimenez. Images: Shutterstock.

Compliant with *The Roman Missal, Third Edition*. Printed in the United States of America. 20 19 18 17 16 / 5 4 3 2 1. Third Edition.

Journaling

Have participants complete this at home. Encourage them to share their symbols at the next session. Consider bringing blank nametags for this purpose.

Closing Prayer

Lord, you have created us with the gift of many senses: smell, taste, touch, hearing, and seeing. You have also created us to know you, love you, and serve you. Indeed, we are wonderfully made. Thank you for the gift of this church and for the objects and symbols we encounter here that bring all our senses, our whole selves, closer to you. Increase in our hearts a love and gratitude for the gift of our senses and for the gifts we find in this place. Amen.

Looking Ahead

Lesson *Q12 Who Shepherds the Church?* introduces participants to the *people* in the Church, specifically Church leaders. Have participants write down questions they might have for a priest, deacon, or nun in their journal. If a group (in-session) interview is not possible, encourage them to contact an ordained or religious person for the answers.

Q12: Who Shepherds the Church?

Catechism: 871–945

Objectives

Participants will…

- list the levels of ordination (authority) and their respective jurisdictions within the Catholic hierarchy.
- identify the institutional Church as founded in Jesus Christ.
- describe the value and significance of apostolic succession as it relates to Church unity.
- name the first pope (Peter), the current pope, and a few in between.
- recall a few common religious orders and parish ministries and describe their roles.

Leader Meditation

Matthew 16:18–19

Read the passage, then reflect on its meaning with this prayer:

Heavenly Father, you have called me to lead, teach, and guide those seeking knowledge of the Catholic faith. Help me to inspire in them a love for your Church, an obedience to your teachings, and an understanding of their own call to serve. Renew my respect for each member of your Church, especially my pastor, leaders, and parish ministers. Clarify for us the importance of structure and leadership. I ask this in the name of your Son, Jesus, who stands forever as the head of the Church and obedient to you. Amen.

Related *Catholic Updates*

- "Infallibility and Church Authority" (C8803A)
- "How the Spirit Guides the Church" (C0106A)

Leader Preparation

- Read the lesson, this lesson plan, the Scripture passage, and the *Catechism* sections.
- Be familiar with the many terms in this lesson: pope, Holy See, Roman Curia, infallibility, auxiliary (bishop), cardinal, conclave, USCCB, papal nuncio, priest, diocesan priest, religious priest, pastor, associate (pastor), parochial vicar, monsignor, deacon, transitional deacon, permanent deacon, religious (man or woman), (religious) sister, nun, (religious) brother, monk, consecrated (people), laity, pastoral administrator, parish council, DRE/CRE/PA, lector, altar server/acolyte, extraordinary minister of holy Communion, music minister, cantor. Definitions can be found in this guide's glossary.
- Obtain a list of the popes, from St. Peter to today. Consider providing copies for each participant.
- Gather copies of your diocesan newspaper, magazine, or another Catholic publication following Church news and life. Provide a list of links or web addresses to these and other such sources. Three global resources are the Vatican's (Holy See's) website, Zenit, and Catholic News Service.
- If you haven't already, gather names and contact information for various parish ministries.

Welcome

Welcome participants as they arrive. If you have them, offer blank nametags or cards on which they can draw or write their Catholic symbol from the last session. You may also go around the room and have each participant describe his or her symbol and why it was chosen. Begin promptly.

Opening Scripture

Matthew 16:18–19

Light the candle and read the passage aloud. It describes Jesus' commissioning of Peter as the foundation of his church. Encourage participants to reflect on Jesus' words and to consider how they relate to Church leadership throughout this session.

> "In the Church there is diversity of ministry but unity of mission. To the apostles and their successors Christ has entrusted the office of teaching, sanctifying, and governing in his name and by his power."
>
> CCC 873; see *Decree on the Apostolate of the Laity*, 2

In Short:

- Christ is the head of the Church.
- Those who lead the Church do so with a spirit of *service*.
- We trace our Church leaders back to Peter and the apostles.

Who Shepherds the Church?

Who affects your daily life the most? Certainly your spouse or boss plays a large part in determining your focus, time, and efforts. But friends, coworkers, children, and parents can also change the course of a day, week, project, or event, propelling you forward or turning your attention to something unexpected.

Any time people live or work together, they establish roles and responsibilities to clarify how decisions will be made and work accomplished. This can happen casually, as with roommates, or formally, as within a business. The Church also benefits from organization; its hierarchy and various roles serve the whole of God's people. Following Jesus' example, those who lead the Church are to do so with a spirit of *service*.

> *"If I, therefore, the master and teacher, have washed your feet, you ought to wash one another's feet. I have given you a model to follow, so that as I have done for you, you should also do."*
>
> *John 13:14–15*

- *How is your workplace or living arrangement structured?*
- *How do you make decisions, divide tasks, and work together?*

The Pope

Christ is the head of the Church, and all Christians are united in him. Before ascending to heaven, Jesus gave his apostles special roles and authority in order to continue his mission on earth. Catholics believe these roles and authority have been passed down through the centuries.

In particular, Jesus gave the Apostle Simon Peter a position of ultimate authority and leadership among Jesus' followers. After Peter's martyrdom in Rome, a successor was chosen, inheriting his title of "rock" on which the Church is built (Matthew 16:18). Today, the **pope**, as bishop of Rome, is looked upon as Peter's successor, the recognized leader of the Catholic Church on earth.

The pope also inherits Peter's responsibility to serve the whole Church and the faith that has been handed down. Acting in union with all the bishops, the pope preserves and spreads Christ's teaching as revealed in Scripture, sacred tradition, and the ongoing unfolding of divine revelation. His authority and governance come from the **Holy See** (sometimes *Apostolic* or *Roman See*), which includes the **Roman Curia**—Vatican officials and offices who assist him in the day-to-day handling of Church matters and resources.

ADULTS

CCC 871–945

Who Shepherds the Church?

Have participants name groups to which they belong—immediate and extended families, company departments or committees, social clubs, volunteer groups, athletic leagues, and so on. Ask, "How do you function or relate within these groups, within your home and place of employment?" Discuss the roles and responsibilities within these groups.

Ask, "Why do groups need a leader?" Discuss the importance of having structure and leadership (rules and guidelines) within organizations and societies.

Discuss how these things contribute to the unity and continuity of the organization.

Remind them that authority can be formally granted or naturally occurring. Explain that whether in a business or family, it is natural for founders and parents to hold sway, but such persons must take the common good into account. As employees, stakeholders, and children gain knowledge, experience, and maturity, they will rightly play a greater part, but never dominate the proper leader(s). This analogy is easily understood in the context of the workplace and government.

Discuss each title and role in the lesson, identifying the respective individual within your diocese or parish as you go. Display an image or photograph so participants can put a face to each name.

The Pope

Distribute a list of the popes to illustrate the unbroken line of apostolic succession. Highlight the first few, some recent popes, and notable names in between.

Peter and Church Authority

Work through the passages during the session, sharing the responses below as needed:

- Matthew 16:13–20

("You are Peter, and upon this rock I will build my church…") This passage witnesses to Jesus' institution of the papacy and conferral of highest authority to Peter.

- John 1:40–42

("You are Simon the son of John; you will be called Cephas…") Here Jesus (re)names Simon *Peter*, meaning *the rock* (or foundation of the Church).

- John 21:15–17

In this resurrection account, Peter reverses his threefold denial with a threefold affirmation of love. Jesus replies to each instance with a command to "Feed my sheep" (v. 17). This affirms Peter's role and marks it as one of servant leadership.

- Acts 1:15–16, 21–26

("Therefore, it is necessary that one of the men who accompanied us the whole time…become with us a witness to his resurrection.") This passage recounts how Peter guided the disciples in the process of selecting Judas' successor.

- Acts 10:9–42

("When Peter entered, Cornelius met him and, falling at his feet, paid him homage….'We are all here in the presence of God to listen to all that you have been commanded by the Lord.'") In this account, Peter receives a vision and is sent to the house of Cornelius to proclaim God's acceptance of the Gentiles.

- Acts 15:1–12

("It was decided that Paul, Barnabas, and some of the others should go up to Jerusalem to the apostles….The whole assembly fell silent, and they listened while Paul and Barnabas described the signs and wonders God had worked…") This passage recounts the Council of Jerusalem, in which the necessity of circumcision for Gentile converts is authoritatively denied.

Peter and Church Authority

Read and reflect on the Scripture passages below. How does each one illustrate the unique role of Peter (and the popes after him)?

Matthew 16:13–20	John 1:40–42
John 21:15–17	Acts 1:15–16, 21–26
Acts 10:9–42	Acts 15:1–12

Is the Pope Infallible?

It's easy to misunderstand what the Church means by papal infallibility. It does not mean that the pope never makes a mistake. It does not mean that the pope never sins. What **infallibility** does mean is that under these certain specific conditions, the teaching of the pope is preserved from error by the Holy Spirit:

- The pope must be speaking in his capacity as chief leader and shepherd of the Church.
- He must be clearly defining a teaching as being a truth of faith to be accepted by the whole Church.
- The teaching must be concerned with matters of faith or morals.

The more common teachings of the pope (in homilies, speeches, encyclicals, and so on) don't fulfill these conditions. In fact, the total number of infallible statements is very small. One example is the assumption of the Blessed Virgin Mary, declared in 1950 by Pope Pius XII. Nevertheless, Catholics give due respect to all the teachings of the pope, whether infallible or not.

The Bishops

Peter was only one of the twelve apostles Jesus appointed "to preach and to have authority to drive out demons" (Mark 3:14–15). Catholics teach that the bishops are the successors to these remaining apostles. Through the sacrament of holy orders (ordination), the bishops continue Christ's mission and the work of the apostles and remain in communion with the pope in Rome.

In a large diocese, an **auxiliary bishop** may assist with sacramental and administrative duties.

The pope designates some members of the clergy as **cardinals**. They may vote in the election of a new pope until the age of eighty in a private, prayerful meeting called a **conclave**.

Conferences of bishops and their agencies express and apply Catholic teaching to important religious and social topics within a specific country, region, or culture. Examples are the United States Conference of Catholic Bishops (**USCCB**) and the Canadian Conference of Catholic Bishops (CCCB).

A **papal nuncio** is an archbishop who acts as the official Vatican delegate to a country. He holds the diplomatic rank of ambassador. In the U.S. and Canada, he also functions as a facilitator between these countries' bishops and the Vatican offices in Rome.

- *What qualities make a good leader?*

The Bishops

Pass out copies of a diocesan or other Church publication or display an online or digital version. Identify some of the titles, offices, and key individuals within it.

Priests

> *"Go, therefore, and make disciples of all nations, baptizing them in the name of the Father, and of the Son, and of the holy Spirit, teaching them to observe all that I have commanded you."*
>
> Matthew 28:19–20

Bishops ordain **priests** as coworkers in their mission. A **diocesan priest** is attached to a specific diocese under the authority of the local bishop. A **religious priest** is a member of a religious community and may work in various parts of the world at the invitation of local bishops.

A **pastor** is the bishop's direct representative to a parish. Larger parishes may also have an **associate pastor** (or **parochial vicar**). **Monsignor** is an honorary title given to a priest in recognition of his contributions to the life of the Church.

Deacons

Finding themselves in need of assistants, the apostles said, "Brothers, select from among you seven reputable men, filled with the Spirit and wisdom, whom we shall appoint to this task" (Acts 6:3). The apostles prayed and laid hands on the chosen men.

Today, this is the ministry of a **deacon** ("servant" in Greek), an ordained member of the clergy. A deacon can be **transitional** (a step on the path to priesthood) or **permanent**. Permanent deacons may be married but only if they were married at the time of ordination.

- *Is there a deacon at your local parish? What are his duties and responsibilities?*

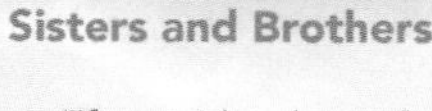

Sisters and Brothers

> *"If you wish to be perfect, go, sell what you have and give to [the] poor....Then come, follow me."*
>
> Matthew 19:21

When the rich young man heard Jesus say these words, "he went away sad, for he had many possessions" (19:22), but others answer Jesus' call and follow Christ as **religious** priests, brothers, or sisters. Examples of religious institutes are the Order of Friars Minor (Franciscans), the Society of Jesus (Jesuits), and the Congregation of the Most Holy Redeemer (Redemptorists). Religious take vows of poverty, chastity, and obedience in order to follow Christ more faithfully.

Some people use the word nun to describe all women in religious institutes. The more appropriate title is **sister**. A **nun** is a sister who belongs to a cloistered (secluded and contemplative) order and resides in a monastery.

A **brother** is a nonordained member of a religious order of men. Priests and brothers in monastic orders are referred to as **monks**. Some religious communities include laypersons and deacons. All men and women, religious or lay, who profess vows of poverty, chastity (in the form of celibacy or perpetual virginity), and obedience are called **consecrated**.

The Laity

Baptized Catholics who aren't ordained make up the **laity** of the Church. Laypeople live out their baptism by bringing the presence of Christ to the world and striving for holiness in their daily lives. Lay adults serve God in marriage or in the single life.

> *"The laity are called in a special way to make the Church present and operative in those places and circumstances where only through them can it become the salt of the earth..."*
>
> Dogmatic Constitution on the Church (Lumen Gentium), 33.

The Laity

Emphasize the importance of the laity, the Church's foundation. Explain that like all organizations, the Church needs not only leaders but also active and dedicated members. Without the faithful, the Church would not exist and could not reach the greater (secular) world.

Parish Ministries

List or brainstorm some ways that anyone can serve the Church. This should not be limited to parish ministries but include Mass attendance, charitable donations, and assisting at home, at work, and through outside agencies and volunteer organizations. Emphasize that everyone, in some way, can (and should) freely share their talents and time with others.

Who's Who?

Allow participants and sponsors to respond aloud if they know the person by name or description. Provide any remaining names, titles, and key ministries. If completing outside of the session, direct participants to the best sources and contacts.

INQUIRY · JOURNEY OF FAITH

Parish Ministries

"To each individual the manifestation of the Spirit is given for some benefit."

1 Corinthians 12:7

According to St. Paul, the people in the Church are responsible for teaching, mighty deeds, healing, assistance, even administration (1 Corinthians 12:28). These roles appear in various titles and positions within a parish, such as:

- **Pastoral Administrator**: In the absence of a full-time pastor, this person handles the pastoral care of the parish that doesn't involve celebrating the sacraments.
- **Parish Council**: This advisory body is made up of elected or appointed people who assist the pastor in the administrative and spiritual life of the parish.
- **Director / Coordinator of Religious Education** or **Pastoral Associate**: These men and women manage the religious formation of parish members. They provide resources and programs for spiritual growth and development.
- **Lectors**: These liturgical ministers read from Scripture (except the Gospel) at Mass and other liturgies.
- **Altar Servers** or **Acolytes**: These people assist at the altar during Mass.
- **Extraordinary Ministers of holy Communion**: These trained laypeople assist the clergy in distributing the Eucharist during Mass and may take Communion to the sick and homebound.
- **Music Ministers**: These liturgical ministers include the organist and instrumentalists as well as singers. The **cantor** may lead the songs, especially the Responsorial Psalm at Mass.

Who's Who?

For each title or ministry below, identify who serves in that role for your parish.

RCIA coordinator, director, or team leader:

Director of Religious Education:

Lector(s):

Extraordinary Minister(s) of holy Communion:

Music or choir director:

How do you already serve God's people and Church in your daily life?

What Catholic ministries or parish groups interest you?

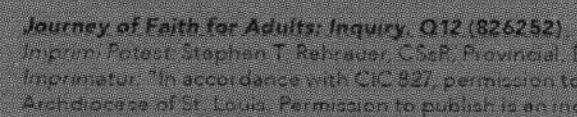

Journey of Faith for Adults: Inquiry, Q12 (826252)
Imprimi Potest: Stephen T. Rehrauer, CSsR, Provincial, Denver Province, the Redemptorists.
Imprimatur: "In accordance with CIC 827, permission to publish has been granted on March 7, 2016, by the Most Reverend Edward M. Rice, Auxiliary Bishop, Archdiocese of St. Louis. Permission to publish is an indication that nothing contrary to Church teaching is contained in this work. It does not imply any endorsement of the opinions expressed in the publication; nor is any liability assumed by this permission."

Contributing Writers: Fr. Gary Ziuraitis, CSsR; Fr. Daniel L. Lowery, CSsR; Fr. Michael Henesy, CSsR; Rosemary Gallagher; Terry Matz. Editors of 2016 edition: Denise Bossert, Julia DiSalvo, and Joan McKamey. Design: Lorena Mitre Jimenez. Images: Shutterstock.

Printed in the United States of America. 20 19 18 17 16 / 5 4 3 2 1 Third Edition

Journaling

Remind participants that they already have a vocation (marriage or single life) and a form of service in their career or volunteer activities. The mystagogy lessons will assist them in determining their specific call(s) to parish life and Christian stewardship, which need not be ministerial or liturgical at this point.

Closing Prayer

Request petitions from the group, and then close with a prayerful reading of Ephesians 4:11–16, which describes the need for ministries within the Church.

Looking Ahead

Lesson *Q13 The Church as Community*, explores how Catholics view "Church"—not simply as an institution or building but as a living body (of people) with diverse and collaborating parts. Instruct participants to read a few articles on the people and events of the Church within their diocese, nation, and the Church around the world.

Q13: The Church as Community

Catechism: 748–810

Objectives

Participants will…

- describe the "Church" as not only a visible, formal institution but also a living and united people of God.
- recognize all Christians as members of the Church—Christ's Mystical Body—with corresponding roles and duties.
- recognize that the Holy Spirit guides the Church to the fullness of truth and protects the deposit of faith from corruption and destruction.

Leader Meditation

John 14:15–31

The Church founded by Jesus continues through the guidance of the Holy Spirit, who dwells in every member. To understand the unity and power of the universal Church, we must first believe that it is ultimately guided by the Spirit working through its diverse members. Though individuals make mistakes and are sometimes misguided, the People of God—as Church—do not wander aimlessly. In particular, verse 26 reminds us that we are being sent in his name and the Holy Spirit will give us what we need to share the good news of the gospel.

Related *Catholic Update*

"Many Faces, One Church: The Blessing and Challenge of Diversity" (C1412A)

Leader Preparation

- Read the lesson, this lesson plan, the Scripture passage, and the *Catechism* sections.
- Be familiar with the terms: Church, Mystical Body of Christ. Definitions can be found in this guide's glossary.
- Read Pope Francis' general audience talk of June 18, 2014, available on the Vatican's website. It is a beautiful description of the Church as a people united in and founded by Jesus, but formed throughout the Old Testament, beginning with God's covenant with Abraham. Short quotes may be shared with participants.

Welcome

Welcome each person as he or she enters the room. Invite participants to share new information and findings from their reading, research, and the previous session. Begin promptly.

Opening Scripture

John 14:15–31

Explain that this passage describes Jesus' promise of the Holy Spirit as leader and guide. Jesus has given us the Spirit to watch over his Church. Point out that the Church is not a building but a people bound together by faith in Christ and led by the Spirit. Now light the candle and read the passage aloud. Have participants consider what peace knowledge (of the truth), authority, and obedience might provide during the session. If insights result, participants may record them in their journals.

"The word 'church' designates the liturgical assembly, but also the local community or the whole universal community of believers. These three meanings are inseparable. "The Church" is the People that God gathers in the whole world. She exists in local communities and is made real as a liturgical, above all a Eucharistic, assembly. She draws her life from the word and the Body of Christ and so herself becomes Christ's Body."

CCC 752

Q13 INQUIRY

In Short:

- The Church is both an institution and a living body.
- Christians are to live as Christ's body in the world.
- The Holy Spirit faithfully guides the Church to the truth.

The Church as Community

What do you think of when you hear the word *church*? You might have thought of a building or the pope and bishops. Perhaps you thought of your RCIA group or the Mass.

The *word* church has many different meanings. For Catholics, however, church is more than a building or a group of people or a liturgy. The truth is expressed at the beginning of Mass: "The grace of our Lord Jesus Christ, and the love of God, and the communion of the Holy Spirit be with you all" *(The Roman Missal, Third Edition).*

The unity of Christians lies in the Trinity. The Church is people united, not by a building or a hierarchy or an organization, but by someone.

The Second Vatican Council declares that the Church shines forth as "a people made one with the unity of the Father, the Son, and the Holy Spirit" (Dogmatic Constitution on the Church *[Lumen Gentium]*, 4). The Church is the community of all those who have been drawn into the life of God "by faith and Baptism" (*CCC* 804) and the continuing presence of Christ leading them to a united vision of God—a people acting as one through the Holy Spirit dwelling in their hearts.

> *"By Baptism the Christian participates in the grace of Christ, the Head of his Body. As an 'adopted son' he can henceforth call God 'Father,' in union with the only Son. He receives the life of the Spirit who breathes charity into him and who forms the Church."*
>
> *CCC 1997*

Read the Scripture passages below and identify how the Church is described:

Colossians 1:18	1 Peter 2:9–10
Ephesians 2:19–20	1 Corinthians 3:9
1 Timothy 3:15	Galatians 3:28

Why Do We Need the Church?

We are made in the image and likeness of God. Since God is a loving community of Father, Son, and Holy Spirit, we are created to be in community as well.

Jesus came to draw us into the "community love" of the Trinity. Jesus lived, died, and rose to bring all people into one family (John 10:16–18). At the Last Supper, he asked us to love one another as he loves us (John 15:12) and prayed that we would be one, as he and the Father are one (17:20–21).

CCC 748–810

ADULTS

The Church as Community

Emphasize that the Trinity is the model and source of the Church's unity. If participants question or are curious about the mandate of baptism, share the Scripture passages that serve as the foundation of that teaching (Mark 16:16, Acts 2:38, Acts 19:17–1, Acts 10:44–48, Romans 6:3–4).

Read each passage in response to "How is the Church described in Scripture?" aloud. Explain how each of these highlight some Catholic understanding of the Church as needed:

- Colossians 1:18

("[The Son] is the head of the body, the church. He is the beginning, the firstborn from the dead…") Christ is the head of the Church.

- 1 Peter 2:9–10

("But you are 'a chosen race, a royal priesthood, a holy nation, a people of his own…'") The Church is God's (chosen) people.

- Ephesians 2:19–20

("You are no longer strangers and sojourners, but you are fellow citizens with the holy ones and members of the household of God, built upon the foundation of the apostles and prophets…") Every member of the Church is a precious child of God and called to holiness. The Church was established in the New Covenant and maintains the apostolic tradition.

- 1 Corinthians 3:9

("We are God's co-workers; you are God's field, God's building.") Christians are called to seek God's kingdom and to help bring it to fulfillment.

- 1 Timothy 3:15

("…the household of God, which is the church of the living God, the pillar and foundation of truth.") God is present and active in the Church, through which all can find the truth.

- Galatians 3:28

("There is neither Jew nor Greek, there is neither slave nor free person, there is not male and female; for you are all one in Christ Jesus.") Christ extends salvation to all humanity.

Why Do We Need the Church?

Acknowledge that many claim that they do not need "church" and that they "pray better" alone. Ask participants why the faith community is important to them. Have sponsors and team members add their own insights as to why the Church is important to them and to society as a whole. Previous lessons and the many scriptural references in this lesson address concerns surrounding the need for (and benefits to) communal worship.

The Mystical Body

Emphasize the importance of every part of the human body and every member of the Body of Christ. Have participants respond to the lesson's question, "What gifts do you bring to the body of Christ?" See Romans 12:3–8 for a scriptural reference.

Jesus formed the community of believers into the sign of his continuing presence on earth: "Where two or three are gathered together in my name, there am I in the midst of them" (Matthew 18:20). When Saul was persecuting Christians after Jesus had ascended into heaven, he encountered the risen Christ asking him, "Why are you persecuting me?" (Acts 9:4). Saul (later called Paul) came to understand the unity between Christ and believers: in persecuting Christians, he had been persecuting Jesus himself.

> *"There are many parts, yet one body....*
> *If [one] part suffers, all the parts suffer with it; if one part is honored, all the parts share its joy. You are Christ's body, and individually parts of it."*
>
> *1 Corinthians 12:20, 27-27*

What Did Paul Mean by Calling the Church Christ's Body?

Paul uses the terms *body of Christ* and *church* interchangeably. **Church** (*Ekklesia* in Greek) is an assembly of people called forth, "the people of God." Christ calls forth believers to share him with the world, saying: "This is how all will know that you are my disciples, if you have love for one another" (John 13:35). The Church must continue the love of Christ on earth and mirror the love of the Trinity.

Christ put a great deal of trust in his apostles and in us. He depends on all Christians to continue his work. His ongoing mission through the Church depends on his followers being Christ to the world. Before Jesus was crucified, he lived in his own mortal body through which he could speak, listen, touch, forgive, heal, comfort, share, pray, love, unite, and bless. Now the Church is his body.

Christ has no body but yours,
No hands, no feet on earth but yours,
Yours are the eyes with which he looks
Compassion on this world,
Yours are the feet with which he walks to do good,
Yours are the hands, with which he blesses all the world.
Yours are the hands, yours are the feet,
Yours are the eyes, you are his body.

St. Teresa of Ávila

Parents raising their children, students attending class, adults at their jobs, priests in their ministries, the elderly in nursing homes—all are the body of Christ by virtue of baptism.

- *What gifts do you bring to the body of Christ?*

The Mystical Body

The **Mystical Body of Christ** describes the whole Church, united with one another and with Christ as its head. In addition to calling the Church the Body of Christ, we use the terms People of God, Bride of Christ, and Temple of the Holy Spirit (*CCC* 781–798).

Each member is uniquely part of the body of Christ. All Christians are called to work together as one, just as the parts of the human body work together. Although made up of individuals, members of the Church don't live for themselves alone but for the entire body of Christ. In the celebration of the Mass, Catholics are joined in prayer as one body.

INQUIRY | JOURNEY OF FAITH

Did Jesus Intend to Start a Church?

The first generation of Christians believed that Christ intended to establish a Church (Matthew 16:18) with leaders who would make decisions ratified by God (Matthew 18:18). Christ gave them ritual observances (Luke 22:19), rules of conduct (Matthew 6:21–22), and guidelines for marriage (Mark 10:11).

We know Jesus wanted to build a community because he gathered disciples around him. He called them his "little flock" and spoke to them of his kingdom. He taught them the message they were to proclaim and appointed twelve of them as apostles. But he didn't leave a clear plan for how to continue this work after his ascension into heaven.

The apostles drew upon Jesus' sayings, teachings, and commands as well as his lived example. His death and resurrection were vindication and approval of all he'd done. Finally, he sent the Holy Spirit to remind them of all he said and did to guide their journey even as times changed and new questions emerged in the area of faith and morals.

How Does God Guide the Church?

Since the Church on earth is made up of human beings who aren't perfect, it's to be expected that the Church will be less than perfect. "The Church... will receive its perfection only in the glory of heaven" (*Lumen Gentium*, 48).

Jesus knew that those who would represent him were subject to failure. Peter denied him three times, but Jesus, after his resurrection, gave Peter a threefold commission to care for his flock (John 21:15–18). The apostles ran away when Jesus was arrested, yet he appeared to them after his resurrection and sent them to preach the gospel to all nations (Matthew 28:16–20).

The early Church had all the problems found in the Church today. (And indeed, similar problems can be found in any large, human organization.) Scanning through the Acts of the Apostles, readers will find liars and hypocrites (5:1–11), complaints of unfairness (6:1), use of religion for personal gain (8:9–24), disagreements about doctrine (15:24), conflicts among Church leaders (15:36–41), and preaching that failed to make an impact (17:22–34). The community in Corinth struggled with questions about pastors' salaries, disorder at worship ceremonies, scandal, and neglect of the poor (1 Corinthians 5—11). All these problems naturally arise when people try to follow Jesus and fall short because of human weakness and sin.

In spite of these challenges and human failures, the Church has been the means through which millions of people in every age and of every class and race have come to know Jesus Christ and his life-giving message. From its ranks, the Church has produced individuals universally recognized for their outstanding goodness and holiness—people like Francis of Assisi, Teresa of Calcutta, Óscar Romero, and Dorothy Day.

At times in the Church's history, some of its members have been unfaithful to the Spirit of God. But the Spirit always remains faithful, leading the Church to the truth. That's why the Church continues to be a sign of Christ's presence in the world and to proclaim his message of love, forgiveness, dignity, joy, hope, and peace.

All members of Christ's body are responsible for making Christ physically present to those among whom they live and work. They carry on the tradition—the gifts, legacy, mission, and truths—they have received. They not only strive to learn about the Church but also endeavor to be the Church, the body of Christ in the world today.

- *How can you make Christ present in the world through your daily life?*

Did Jesus Intend to Start a Church?

Provide examples of the great diversity within the Church to counter concerns that Church membership results in unhealthy conformity—various liturgical rites and languages, worship and prayer styles, ministries and forms of stewardship, and causes for which one can pursue social justice (which encompass both political parties).

Point out that the minimum (universal) requirements for "living Catholic"—known as the "precepts of the Church"—are very few and mainly surround the Mass and Eucharist (*CCC* 2041–43).

How Does God Guide the Church?

Remind participants that like all institutions, the Church makes mistakes. Though guided by the Spirit, Church leaders are human, subject to the same temptations of greed, power, and self-indulgence. The mission of the whole Church is to better discern God's will through careful attention to Jesus' teachings and openness to the Spirit's promptings. When we fail or fall short, we should seek mercy and reconciliation and make amends. When our Christian brothers and sisters are in danger of sin or abandoning faith, we should offer gentle, private correction and encouragement in the hope of God's eternal love (Matthew 18:15–20).

Reaffirm the Church's holiness despite the imperfections of its members. Clarify that this holiness comes from Christ's presence within it and from the Spirit who sustains it, not from anything any person has done or not done. Earlier lessons discuss Church authority and papal infallibility as related to this matter. Quote or discuss the references to Scripture as needed:

- Acts 5:1–11

("Ananias, why has Satan filled your heart so that you lied to the holy Spirit?")

- Acts 6:1

("The Hellenists complained against the Hebrews because their widows were being neglected in the daily distribution.")

- Acts 8:9–24

("May your money perish with you, because you thought that you could buy the gift of God with money.")

- Acts 15:24

("We have heard that some of our number [who went out] without any mandate from us have upset you with their teachings and disturbed your peace of mind.")

- Acts 15:36–41

("So sharp was their disagreement that they separated.")

- Acts 17:22–34

("Some began to scoff, but others said, 'We should like to hear you on this some other time.'")

- 1 Corinthians 5–11

("It is widely reported that there is immorality among you.... When you sin in this way against your brothers and wound their consciences, weak as they are, you are sinning against Christ.")

JOURNEY OF FAITH INQUIRY

There are many inspiring examples of Catholics today actively living as part of Christ's body.

Search your parish bulletin, diocesan publication, or a national Catholic media site for an example of a person or organization that:

1. offers their particular gifts and talents for the greater good.
2. illustrates Christ's presence in the world.
3. reflects the love of the Trinity.
4. works for reconciliation and/or greater unity within the Church.

Share your findings with the rest of the group.

Journey of Faith for Adults: Inquiry, Q13 (826252)
Imprimi Potest: Stephen T. Rehrauer, CSsR, Provincial, Denver Province, the Redemptorists.
Imprimatur: "In accordance with CIC 827, permission to publish has been granted on March 7, 2016, by the Most Reverend Edward M. Rice, Auxiliary Bishop, Archdiocese of St. Louis. Permission to publish is an indication that nothing contrary to Church teaching is contained in this work. It does not imply any endorsement of the opinions expressed in the publication; nor is any liability assumed by this permission."

Contributing writers: Fr. Oscar Lukefahr, CM; Fr. Joe Morin, CSsR; Fr. Christopher Gaffney, CSsR; Fr. John Trenchard, CSsR. Editors of 2016 edition: Denise Bossert, Julia DiSalvo, and Joan McKamey. Design: Lorena Mitre Jimenez. Images: Shutterstock.

Printed in the United States of America. 20 19 18 17 16 / 5 4 3 2 1. Third Edition.

Liguori PUBLICATIONS
A Redemptorist Ministry

Journaling

Remind participants to write their responses to the prompts in their prayer journal.

Activity

Have participants complete this activity on their own. Provide copies or issues of publications as necessary, and invite them to share their findings at the next session.

Closing Prayer

Ask the group to state any petitions or special intentions, then read aloud the reassuring words of Matthew 18:19–20:

"Again, [amen,] I say to you, if two of you agree on earth about anything for which they are to pray, it shall be granted to them by my heavenly Father. For where two or three are gathered together in my name, there am I in the midst of them."

Looking Ahead

Lesson *Q14 Mary*, continues and deepens our study of the Church beyond those currently living on earth or serving your local diocese. In preparation for this lesson, have the participants list some titles, apparitions, or images of Mary and research a few. Displaying them together will illustrate the Church's great diversity even within our united faith.

Q14: Mary

Catechism: 963–975

Objectives

Participants will...

- distinguish between veneration and intercession (in regard to Mary and the saints).
- recognize how major teachings about Mary are tied to teachings about Jesus.
- name several key titles of Mary and their meanings.
- gain comfort and confidence in honoring, reflecting on, and praying to Mary.

Leader Meditation

Luke 1:46–55

Lord, may my life magnify your presence here on earth. Like Mary, may I serve your people with humility and compassion. Like a loving mother, may I care for the people under my guidance. May I lead and instruct them with patience and understanding. Amen.

Related *Catholic Update*

"In Search of the Real Mary" (C0105A)

Leader Preparation

- Read the lesson, this lesson plan, the Scripture passage, and the *Catechism* sections.
- Be familiar with the terms: venerate, saint, intercession, worship, dogma, apparition. Definitions can be found in this guide's glossary.
- Gather images of Mary and Marian icons, apparitions, and related churches and shrines.
- Gather copies of various Marian prayers and devotions to share with each participant and sponsor.
- If possible, obtain a copy of John Michael Talbot's song "Holy Is His Name" for the closing prayer.

Welcome

Welcome each participant as he or she arrives. Invite them to share new information and findings from their reading, research, and the previous session. Begin promptly.

Opening Scripture

Luke 1:46–55

Light the candle and read the passage aloud. Explain that this passage is known as Mary's *Magnificat*. In this passage, the word *magnifies* means "glorifies." Mary gives God her highest praise and exclusive adoration. In order to magnify God, she subjects herself completely to God's will. Ask participants, "How do you honor important people in your life?" Affirm their responses and point out how such instances strengthen others and bring glory to God's creation and Church.

"Mary's role in the Church is inseparable from her union with Christ and flows directly from it. 'This union of the mother with the Son in the work of salvation is made manifest from the time of Christ's virginal conception up to his death.'" CCC 964

Q14

INQUIRY

In Short:

- Catholics honor Mary as Jesus' first and most perfect disciple.
- Mary intercedes for us as Jesus' Mother and Mother of the Church.
- Mary's titles express aspects of her relationship with Jesus and with us.

Mary

Jesus is at the center of the Catholic faith. This lesson is about Mary, his Mother, one of the most honored people in the faith. When Mary was asked to be the mother of the Son of God, she responded: "May it be done to me according to your word" (Luke 1:38). Mary accepted God's will for her life. She became the Christ bearer, the one through whom Jesus, our hope for salvation, entered the world, making our redemption possible.

So it makes sense that those who confess Jesus as their Lord would also respect and **venerate** (honor and revere) Mary. If we love Jesus, we love his mother because of her important role in his life. "Mary's role in the Church is inseparable from her union with Christ and flows directly from it" (CCC 964).

> *"Most blessed are you among women, and blessed is the fruit of your womb."*
>
> Luke 1:42

- *Think of a woman who has influenced your life. What makes her so special to you?*

Who First Honored Mary?

God the Father honored Mary by choosing her and allowing the fullness of divinity to take human form within her. The angel Gabriel, sent from God, announced: "Hail, favored one! The Lord is with you" (Luke 1:28). This greeting has become the first part of the Hail Mary prayer.

Jesus, the Son of God, honored Mary. He chose her to be his mother. At the beginning of his public ministry, he changed water into wine at the wedding feast at Cana because she requested it (John 2:1–11).

The first disciples honored Mary. She prayed with them as they waited for the coming of the Spirit (Acts 1:14). Just as Jesus was born of Mary, so the Christian Church was born at Pentecost with Mary present.

The early Church honored Mary. Saint Luke honored Mary in the stories of the annunciation, visitation, and birth of Christ. Mary was a popular figure for devotion among the first Christians. As early as AD 150 in the catacombs of Rome, people painted pictures of Mary holding the baby Jesus.

> *"Never be afraid of loving the Blessed Virgin too much. You can never love her more than Jesus did."*
>
> St. Maximilian Kolbe

CCC 963–975

ADULTS

Mary

Emphasize Mary's humanity throughout the session. Her willingness to say "yes" to the difficult things God asked of her is what makes her so special.

Clarify the difference between worship and veneration.

Ask the participants for examples of how they can say "yes" to God in difficult or challenging situations.

Who First Honored Mary?

Remind participants that dedicating churches to Mary's name and titles, and praying with her image in sacramentals and religious artwork, are ways to guide the faithful to Christ. Mary should never be an object of worship.

How Do Catholics Honor Mary?

Encourage participants to consider Mary as a precious gift from God and their maternal intercessor. Like God, we come to know and respect Mary more by spending time in communication with her.

What Is the Immaculate Conception?

Remind participants that this title refers to Mary's conception (in Anne's womb), not Jesus'. Confusing even to some Catholics is that the Church celebrates this holy day of obligation in the midst of Advent (December 8). It may help to share that the feast of Mary's nativity is September 8, nine months after the feast of the Immaculate Conception.

Expand on Mary's unique role as the "new Eve" if there's time (see *CCC* 411, 489, 511, 726, 975, 2618, 2853). This discussion could continue into a longer exploration of Mary's role and title as Ark of the New Covenant (see Deuteronomy 10:8–9; 1 Chronicles 15:1–3, 14–15; 1 Chronicles 17:1–4, 10b–14; 1 Samuel 4:6–7; and 2 Samuel 6).

How Do Catholics Honor Mary?

Catholics honor Mary by taking her as our Mother and learning to imitate her. Mary accepted God's will completely. She was the first and most perfect of Christ's disciples, making her first among the **saints** (holy people in heaven). She shows us how to follow Jesus and share his gospel with others. In honoring and imitating Mary, we praise and thank God for all he has done through her.

Catholics also honor Mary by requesting her **intercession**, asking her to pray to God for us or to join her prayer with ours. Is it necessary to do this? No. We can pray directly to God. By calling on Mary's intercession, however, we have someone praying for and with us who is very close to Jesus.

Does devotion to Mary replace dedication to God? No. Mary is a created being and a servant of the Lord. She points us to Jesus, our Savior and Redeemer. In praying to Mary, Catholics don't **worship** (adore or pay homage to) her. God alone is worthy of worship. We do, however, honor her for her important role in our salvation and for her acceptance of God's will.

> *"Mary hears the word of God and keeps it. In this, she is, as Pope Paul VI called her in* Marialis Cultus, *'our sister' in faith."*
>
> *Elizabeth Johnson, CSJ,* In Search of the Real Mary

What Is the Immaculate Conception?

The **dogma** of the Immaculate Conception proclaims that Mary was free of original sin from the moment of *her* conception in her mother's womb and free of all personal sin throughout her life. In other words, God saved her from the inheritance of Adam and Eve's sin and prevented her from the corruption and burden of guilt. This allowed Mary to be the spotless vessel that received and carried the perfect and divine Son of God.

Our Mother of Perpetual Help

Our Lady of Guadalu

Dogma: a doctrine (teaching) of the Church that cannot be disputed or denied. Its belief and acceptance by the faithful is necessary for salvation.

This sinless state both recalls our original existence in the Garden of Eden and foreshadows eternal life in God's kingdom. Just as Eve symbolizes our fallen human nature, Mary symbolizes the redeemed nature of the saints in heaven. For this reason, the Church refers to her as the "new Eve."

What Is the Assumption of Mary?

Mary's gifts and graces didn't end with her last breath. Pope Pius XII defined the dogma of the assumption in these words: "the Immaculate Mother of God, the ever Virgin Mary, having completed the course of her earthly life, was assumed body and soul into heavenly glory" (*Munificentissimus Deus*, 44, November 1, 1950).

We, too, are meant to be with God in heaven one day—body and soul. Just as Jesus' resurrection is our sign of hope, Mary's assumption is the first fruit of God's promise that the faithful will share in that resurrection.

...pe and Pope Francis Our Lady of Lourdes

Why Do Catholics Call Mary Ever-Virgin?

Mary conceived Jesus through the power of the Holy Spirit (Luke 1:34–35). Catholic teaching and tradition affirm that Mary remained a virgin after Jesus' birth as well. Mary's call to perpetual virginity enabled her to consecrate herself totally to the love of God and to her son.

Some Bible passages such as Mark 6:3 say that Jesus had siblings. Catholics don't interpret these to mean that Mary bore other children. In some Jewish accounts, all close relatives including cousins were referred to as brothers. A second-century tradition indicates that these were Joseph's children from a previous marriage. In John's Gospel, Jesus entrusted Mary to the beloved disciple (19:26–27). Saint Hilary of Poitiers taught that Jesus wouldn't have done that if Mary had other sons (*Commentary on Matthew*, 1:4 [AD 354]).

Why Do We Call Mary the Mother of God?

Mary is the Mother of God because Jesus is God, and his divine and human natures can't be separated. This doesn't mean Mary was the source of his divine nature; he received only his human nature from her. As the second person of the Trinity, the Son has existed for all eternity. Yet at the moment of his Incarnation, the Son became both human and divine in Jesus. Since Mary is the Mother of a divine person, it's proper to call her the "Mother of God."

> *"The One whom she conceived as man by the Holy Spirit, who truly became her Son according to the flesh, was none other than the Father's eternal Son, the second person of the Holy Trinity. Hence the Church confesses that Mary is truly 'Mother of God.'"*
>
> *CCC 495*

Read the Gospel passages and quote below. Identify two qualities of Mary. Then reflect on how you can imitate Mary in your own life in your journal.

Luke 1:26–38 (the annunciation)
Luke 1:39–56 (the visitation)
Luke 2:1–21 (the birth of Jesus)
John 2:1–12 (the wedding at Cana)
John 19:25–27 (standing by the cross)

> *"[Mary] was a woman who did not hesitate to proclaim that God vindicates the humble and the oppressed...a woman of strength, who experienced poverty and suffering, flight and exile...a woman whose action helped to strengthen the apostolic community's faith in Christ (see John 2:1–12), and whose maternal role was extended and became universal on Calvary."*
>
> *Pope Paul VI, Marialis Cultus, 37*

What Is the Assumption of Mary?

Assist participants in beginning the "qualities of Mary" activity by identifying some universal Christian values. Those who complete it during the session may share one quality or way they can imitate Mary this week with the group.

Responses may include but are not limited to:

- Luke 1:26–38

("[Gabriel] said, 'Hail, favored one!...' Mary said, 'Behold, I am the handmaid of the Lord.'") holy, blessed, full of grace, humble, deferential, curious

- Luke 1:39–56

("My spirit rejoices in God my savior....From now on will all ages call me blessed.") joyful, hopeful, prophetic, generous, evangelistic

- Luke 2:1–21

("Mary kept all these things, reflecting on them in her heart.") obedient, persevering, loving, nurturing, reflective, prayerful

- John 2:1–12

("His mother said to the servers, 'Do whatever he tells you.'") perceptive, insightful, persuasive, inspiring

- John 19:25–27

("Jesus saw his mother and the disciple there whom he loved...") faithful, dutiful, accepting, welcoming (to her new "son")

- *Marialis Cultus*

brave, strong, modest

How Is Mary the Mother of the Church?

Give examples of Old Testament matriarchs (Sarah: Genesis 17; Miriam: Exodus 15:20–21, Ruth; Hannah: 1 Samuel 1; Esther) and discuss ways they prefigure Mary and God's divine plan for the Messiah and his mother (see *CCC* 489).

What Are Marian Apparitions?

Display or share images of Mary in various biblical scenes and in her various roles and apparitions. A diverse sampling of biblical paintings, stained glass, gilded icons, statues, and modern photographs will broaden participants' own perspective and understanding.

Distribute some Marian prayers, novenas, litanies, and devotions, if there's time. Read a few out loud slowly so as to allow the words and sentiments to sink in.

JOURNEY OF FAITH INQUIRY

How Is Mary the Mother of the Church?

From the cross, Jesus said to Mary, "Woman, behold, your son" (John 19:26). Then he said to the beloved disciple, "Behold, your mother" (19:27). In that moment, Jesus presents Mary as a mother to all Christian disciples. For this reason, Mary is the "Mother of the Church."

Mary supported and remained with the early Church until she was assumed into heaven. She continues to intercede and care for us today.

What Are Marian Apparitions?

Many trustworthy and holy people have reported **apparitions**, or supernatural visions, of Mary and messages that have been the source of countless blessings. Shrines dedicated to these appearances are visited by millions each year—most notably Our Lady of Guadalupe in Mexico, Lourdes in France, and Fatima in Portugal.

The Catholic Church doesn't require belief in such appearances, but official declarations have stated that certain apparitions and the messages associated with them are worthy of belief and compatible with Catholic doctrine. Scripture affirms that God sent angels as messengers of his word; it's just as reasonable to believe that Jesus could send his Mother.

Hundreds of miracles at Marian shrines have been studied and declared to be beyond medical explanation. Those who study these miracles are amazed at the evident presence of God's power and grace working through the intercession of Mary as well as her maternal affection and care for us.

- *Which Marian apparition most intrigues you? Why?*

Mary responded to God's grace and blessings with humble acceptance, peaceful patience, and joyful praise.

How can you show Mary your gratitude for giving us Jesus?

How can you praise God and spread his salvation in your own life, family, and community?

***Journey of Faith for Adults: Inquiry*, Q14 (826252)**

Imprimi Potest: Stephen T. Rehrauer, CSsR, Provincial, Denver Province, the Redemptorists

Imprimatur: "In accordance with CIC 827, permission to publish has been granted on March 7, 2016, by the Most Reverend Edward M. Rice, Auxiliary Bishop, Archdiocese of St. Louis. Permission to publish is an indication that nothing contrary to Church teaching is contained in this work. It does not imply any endorsement of the opinions expressed in the publication; nor is any liability assumed by this permission."

Contributing writers: Fr. Peter Schineller, SJ; Fr. Patrick Kaler, CSsR; Fr. Oscar Lukefahr, CM; Fr. James Higgins, CSsR. Elizabeth Johnson, CSJ, quotation from *Catholic Update* "In Search of the Real Mary" © 1999 Liguori Publications. Editors of 2016 *Journey of Faith for Adults*: Denise Bossert, Julia DiSalvo, and Joan McKamey. Design: Lorena Mitre Jimenez. Images: Shutterstock and Catholic News Service

Printed in the United States of America. 20 19 18 17 16 / 5 4 3 2 1. Third Edition.

Journaling

Have participants record their responses to the two questions in their journals.

Closing Prayer

Dim the lights and listen to the beautiful lyrics and melody in John Michael Talbot's "Holy Is His Name." If the song is unavailable, pray the *Hail Mary*.

Looking Ahead

Lesson *Q15 The Saints*, presents Church teachings and practices surrounding the saints. Mary is the quintessential saint—holy from the moment of conception and assumed into heaven. Remind participants to complete the "qualities of Mary" activity and to follow through on their planned action.

Have participants gather names, images, or stories of any biblical figure or Catholic saint to whom they feel attracted, connected, or about whom they are curious. Remind them to bring these items to the next session.

Q15: The Saints

Catechism: 946–62, 2683–84

Objectives

Participants will…

- define a saint as a human person who lived in conformity to Christ, demonstrated heroic virtue, now lives in heaven, and is worthy of our honor and able to intercede for us.
- identify the groups of people included in the communion of saints—the faithful on earth, the suffering in purgatory (those on their way to heaven), and the saints in heaven.
- recall the three steps of the canonization process.

Leader Meditation (Prayer)

Lord Jesus, I remember your promise, "I will not leave you orphans." You have sent your Holy Spirit to be with us, to guide us, to lead us to heaven. All who are filled with your Spirit are with us in the communion of saints. Grant that I may always recognize their presence and be guided toward holiness by their example. Help me encourage the people under my guidance to seek out and follow those whom you have sent to teach us and to lead us. Amen.

Related *Catholic Update*

"Saintly Sinners: Flawed but Faithful Models of Holiness" (C1410A)

Leader Preparation

- Read the lesson, this lesson plan, and the *Catechism* sections.
- Be familiar with the terms: holy/holiness, martyr, canonization, communion of saints. Definitions can be found in this guide's glossary.
- Select a brief reading on the life of a saint, such as from *Butler's Lives of the Saints* or another biography, writing, or Catholic encyclopedia. Prepare or gather any additional materials that will aid your presentation.

Welcome

Greet the participants, asking each one the name of the saint he or she explored. Invite them to share any new information, findings, or questions that emerged. Those who brought images or items may display them or pass them around the group. Begin promptly.

Opening Reading

Instead of a Scripture passage, choose a story from the lives of the saints. After the reading, ask, "What makes this person exceptional, heroic, unique, or especially devout or pious?" Ask participants if they can relate to that saint. Remind them that God calls even those who struggle and sin to become saints. We are all called to find our path to holiness. Encourage them to reflect on who they consider holy and worthy of emulation, perhaps from their own life or community, throughout the session.

"The witnesses who have preceded us into the kingdom, especially those whom the Church recognizes as saints, share in the living tradition of prayer by the example of their lives, the transmission of their writings, and their prayer today." CCC 2683

Q15

INQUIRY

In Short:

- The saints are our models for faithful living.
- The communion of saints includes those in heaven, purgatory, and on earth.
- Canonization is the process used to declare someone a saint.

The Saints

Think of someone you consider to be a faithful Christian. Much like the person who came to your mind, the saints are real people who led holy lives. You might not think of people in your life—or yourself!—as *holy.*

The truth is, we're all called to be **holy**; we're all called to be saints. Saints are role models for us. They're examples of the "poor in spirit" whose confidence is in God and who recognize their dependence on God. Jesus calls them "blessed" and promises that "theirs is the kingdom of heaven" (Matthew 5:3).

Most of us won't be officially recognized by the Church as saints, but we are all called to choose God with our lives. In other words, we must be *holy.*

> *"Not all of us can do great things. But we can do small things with great love."*
>
> St. Teresa of Calcutta

All Are Called to Be Saints

The Russian Orthodox word for a saint, *prepodobnia*, means "very, very like." During their lives, saints become "very, very like" Jesus. We are each called to become like Jesus, too.

Maybe you don't think of yourself as holy because you haven't done anything great or are aware of your many sins. That's no excuse. Considered one of the greatest saints, Thérèse of Lisieux, a Carmelite nun who lived in a cloister and died at age twenty-four, is admired in part because of her rejection of things the world saw as important. She simply found holiness in everyday things.

Some saints struggled with their studies while some were scholars. Some saints were married, some divorced, some single, and some members of the clergy or religious communities. Some saints died at twelve years old while some lived 100 years. There are saints from all ethnic and racial backgrounds, saints with disabilities, saints who grew up homeless, and saints who grew up to be kings and queens.

> *"We are all called to be saints. God expects something from each of us that no one else can do."*
>
> Dorothy Day, founder of the Catholic Worker Movement

CCC 946–62, 2683–84

ADULTS

The Saints

Read this quote from Fr. James Martin, SJ: "Some might argue (and some do argue) that all you need is Jesus. And that's true: Jesus is everything, and the saints understood this more than anyone. But God in his wisdom has also given us these companions of Jesus to accompany us along the way, so why not accept the gift of their friendship and encouragement?" (*My Life With the Saints*, 7).

All Are Called to Be Saints

Invite the group to propose a living candidate for beatification and canonization, if there's time. This may be easier for team members and sponsors than participants. Discuss why this person may or may not demonstrate heroic virtue or qualify as a saint.

How Does the Church Choose Saints?

Remind participants that the tradition of honoring the saints has been a part of the Church since its beginning. This has allowed us to benefit from the grace God has worked through them. The lives of the saints help to bridge the gap between what we experience and the spiritual realities we cannot fully sense.

Walk participants briefly through the three-step canonization process if there's time:

1. After a person's death, the local bishop can request a *Cause for Beatification and Canonization* to the Holy See (Vatican). If opened, evidence and testimony of the person's life and virtue is gathered, and he or she is given the title *Servant of God*. This is brought to the Congregation for the Causes of Saints (Roman Curia) for approval. If they agree heroic virtue has been demonstrated, the person is called *Venerable*.

2. Next, a miracle proceeding from the person's intercession must be confirmed. Those involved present their case to their diocese, and the decision is forwarded to the congregation. If the person is shown to have died a true, Christian martyr, the requirement for a miracle could be waived. Once the pope consents, a *beatification* ceremony takes place, and the person is called *Blessed*.

3. A second miracle (or first for martyrs) must occur before canonization is possible.

JOURNEY OF FAITH INQUIRY

How Does the Church Choose Saints?

Honoring saints has been part of Christianity from the very start. This practice came from the longstanding Jewish tradition of honoring prophets and holy people with shrines. Catholics honor Mary, the Mother of Jesus, as greatest among the saints. Many of the first saints were **martyrs**, people who were persecuted and died for their faith.

The pope and bishops oversee the process of **canonization**. The title "saint" tells us a person lived a holy life, is in heaven, and is to be honored by the universal Church. But canonization doesn't make a person a saint; it only recognizes what God has already done. While every canonized saint is holy, not every holy person has been canonized.

The canonization process begins after the death of a Catholic who is considered holy. His or her life is examined for heroic virtue or martyrdom, faithfulness to Church teaching, and reputation for holiness. There must be evidence of miracles after the candidate's death, resulting from a request to the saint for help. These miracles prove that the person is in heaven and can intercede for us.

Isn't Having Images of Saints Idolatry?

Some people think the Catholic use of images and statues of saints is idolatry. But that's not how Catholics think of our devotion to saints. Saints serve as role models of faithful Christian living and intercede for us in prayer. We use images to remind us of their faithful example and their ongoing concern for us.

It's similar to how people keep pictures and mementos as reminders of loved ones, yet most don't worship the items or the individuals. Seeing a statue of St. Thérèse of Lisieux, whose mother died when Thérèse was a child, might help us feel less alone when we're grieving. A picture of St. Francis of Assisi might remind us of his love for God's creation and make us more aware of our environment.

St. Thérèse of Lisieux

St. John Bosco

Why Do Catholics Pray to Saints?

Catholics don't pray to saints as they pray to God. Only God is worthy of worship. One definition of prayer is "earnest petition." When Catholics pray to saints, they're asking the saints to pray for and with them—to *God*.

Have you ever asked anyone to pray for you? If so, the person was likely someone you trust, who understood your problem, or who was close to God. Those are all reasons to ask saints to pray for and with you in times of trouble.

Since saints led holy lives and are close to God in heaven, their prayers are particularly effective. Catholics often ask a specific saint to pray for

The process is similar to before. When the pope approves and canonizes the person (an infallible act), he or she is declared to be a *saint* and worthy of veneration by the whole Church.

Why Do Catholics Pray to Saints?

Explain that the prayers of the saints are efficacious because the saints are with God in heaven and can pray without the distractions and concerns of the world.

St. John Paul II

St. Teresa of Calcutta

Do some research on the patron saint of your occupation, hobby, or nationality. Find a saint who shares your name or whose feast day is on your birthday. Learn about this saint—his or her life, vocation or career, good works, and close companions.

- *Which saint did you choose?*
- *What do you find inspiring about this saint?*

them if they feel he or she has a particular interest in their problem. For example, since St. Monica prayed for twenty years for her son to become a Christian, many people ask her to pray for them if they struggle to persevere in prayer. Saint Monica's prayers were eventually answered: Her son, Augustine, became a saint and a doctor of the Church.

> *"Do not weep for I shall be more useful to you after my death and I shall help you then more effectively than during my life."*
>
> St. Dominic, dying, to his brothers

Communion of Saints

The Church is the body of Christ, united with one another and with Christ as its head. Also called the communion of saints, this assembly or communion includes all of God's holy ones—those in or on their way to heaven and those on earth who choose Christ with their lives.

> *"The communion of saints is the Church."*
>
> *CCC 946*

Guided Meditation

Sit quietly with a saint, perhaps one from this lesson.

Imagine yourself in a beautiful, peaceful setting. What do you see, hear, feel?

Picture a figure walking toward you. As the figure gets closer, you see it's the saint.

What does the saint look like? What is his or her mood or expression?

The saint asks, "What can I do to help?" Tell him or her something that troubles you.

What does the saint say in response?

Imagine the saint hands you a gift from God. What is it?

The two of you pray to God about your concern.

You feel the saint's ongoing love and support as you end your time together.

Communion of Saints

Ask participants, "How do you see yourself fitting into the communion of saints?"

Allow time for each participant to research and select a saint to learn more about before the end of the session. Assist anyone who can't find a patron or isn't sure who to pick. Sponsors are ideal partners in this work.

Explain that in the United States, it is not the norm to give a new name upon initiation or reception into the full communion. Most catechumens and candidates will use their given name as their baptismal (and confirmation) or "saint" name. Studying one's Christian or Catholic namesake will build a stronger connection to the Church. However, if an inquirer is from a culture in which "it is the practice...to give a new name" or the bishop gives special permission, an optional rite is offered during the rite of acceptance or preparation rites on Holy Saturday (*RCIA* 33.4, 73).

Complete the guided meditation during the session if time allows. Set the mood and adjust lighting, seating, and sound(s) accordingly. Read the lines slowly, pausing after each line or question for silent reflection. Use the saint chosen for the opening reading, a saint from the lesson, or another familiar saint. If participants are capable, this meditation can be done individually with a saint of their choosing.

JOURNEY OF FAITH **INQUIRY**

Imagine yourself in a conversation with God as you share with him your answers to the following questions. Record both sides of the conversation in your journal.

Do you want to do God's will? How do you want to be transformed by God?

How can you open yourself more to this saint-making journey?

***Journey of Faith for Adults: Inquiry*, Q15 (826252)**
Imprimi Potest: Stephen T. Rehrauer, CSsR, Provincial, Denver Province, the Redemptorists
Imprimatur: "In accordance with CIC 827, permission to publish has been granted on March 7, 2016, by the Most Reverend Edward M. Rice, Auxiliary Bishop, Archdiocese of St. Louis. Permission to pubish is an indication that nothing contrary to Church teaching is contained in this work. It does not imply any endorsement of the opinions expressed in the publication, nor is any liability assumed by this permission."

Contributing writer: Terry Mats. Quotation from *Catholic Update* "Saintly Sinners: Flawed but Faithful, Models of Holiness" by Kathy Coffey, © 2014 Liguori Publications. Editors of 2016 *Journey of Faith for Adults*: Denise Bossert, Julia DiSalvo, and Joan McKamey. Design: Lorena Mitre Jimenez. Images: Shutterstock and Catholic News Service.

Compliant with *The Roman Missal, Third Edition*.
Printed in the United States of America. 20 19 18 17 16 / 5 4 3 2 1. Third Edition.

Liguori PUBLICATIONS
A Redemptorist Ministry

Journaling

Clarify that the goal of this journaling is to open yourself to God in prayer and to identify ways in which you can more closely follow Christ's teachings in your everyday life. The process of conversion is gradual, and you won't sense all the ways that God is working in and through you—no one does.

Closing Prayer

Prayerfully read these words written by St. Thérèse of Lisieux, "The Little Flower":

But how shall I show my love, since love proves itself by deeds? …The only way I have of proving my love is to strew flowers before Thee—that is to say, I will let no tiny sacrifice pass, no look, no word. I wish to profit by the smallest actions, and to do them for Love. I wish to suffer for Love's sake, and for Love's sake even to rejoice.…I will sing always, even if my roses must be gathered from amidst thorns (Story of a Soul, chapter 11).

Looking Ahead

Have participants reflect on the eternal consequences of personal choices and actions, as well as the promises and blessings of the life and world to come, while researching their saint. Lesson *Q16 Eschatology: The "Last Things"* describes the options after death and how each are related to Christ's judgment and our free will.

Q16: Eschatology: The "Last Things"

Catechism: 668–82, 988–1060

Objectives

Participants will…

- identify heaven and hell (salvation and condemnation) as the only two eternal outcomes.
- describe purgatory as a final purification in preparation for heaven.
- distinguish between personal (particular) judgment—what happens after death—and the Final Judgment, when the current world and age (human history) end to make way for the Second Coming of Christ and fulfillment of the kingdom.

Leader Meditation

1 Peter 1:3–9, 13–16

Examine your conscience and assess where you are on the journey of becoming holy "as he who called you is holy" so as to inherit eternal life. These Scripture passages may help you: Mark 8:34–38, Luke 9:23–27, and Colossians 3:1–17.

Related *Catholic Updates*

- "What It Means to Be 'Saved'" (C8612A)
- "What Is the Kingdom of God?" (C8009A)
- "The 'Last Things': Death, Judgment, Heaven and Hell" (C9305A)
- "How Catholics Understand Grace" (C0010A)

Leader Preparation

- Read the lesson and this lesson plan. The *Catechism* sections listed above will help you especially to respond to questions posed by participants who come from faith traditions that believe in the rapture and interpretations of the "end times" that are not consistent with Catholic teaching. Other participants may not have any prior understanding or concept of the "last things" or believe in an afterlife.
- Be familiar with the terms: eschatology, heaven, hell, free will, purgatory, Second Coming (end times), Final Judgment. Definitions can be found in this guide's glossary.
- Gather or prepare any instructions or details on the rites of acceptance and welcoming for participants who are entering the period of the catechumenate.

Welcome

Greet the members of the group as they arrive. Check for supplies and immediate needs. Solicit questions or comments about the previous session and/or share new information and findings. Begin promptly.

Opening Scripture

1 Peter 1:3–9, 13–16

Light the candle and read the passage aloud. Explain that the baptism the participants are preparing for is the primary means of ensuring one's eternal salvation. Quote the Nicene Creed, if it helps: "I confess one Baptism for the forgiveness of sins and I look forward to the resurrection of the dead." Encourage them to see their presence here as a joy and blessing, a partial inheritance of the graces they will receive later.

> "Christ is Lord of eternal life. Full right to pass definitive judgment on the works and hearts of men belongs to him as redeemer of the world."
>
> CCC 679

Journey of Faith

Q16

INQUIRY

In Short:

- Heaven and hell are our only possible eternal destinies.
- Purgatory is a purification in preparation for heaven.
- Each of us will undergo both a personal judgment and the Final Judgment.

Eschatology: The "Last Things"

Considering our own mortality and what happens after death can be unnerving, scary, and confusing. We only have slivers of understanding about what happens next. But as Christians, we find comfort and hope in our belief that Jesus has conquered death, granted us eternal life, and promised to come again in final triumph over evil. Church teaching on these "last things" is called eschatology.

Eschatology deals with what comes:

- at the end of a person's life.
- at the end of human history and creation.
- at the Second Coming of Christ.

Let's explore the life and afterlife of "Joe" all the way to the Second Coming. Joe's experiences will help us better understand the general eschatology of all humanity and creation.

"For where your treasure is, there also will your heart be."

Luke 12:34

Life, Death, and Particular Judgment

Joe began his journey of faith at baptism. During his life, Joe had opportunities to respond to God's offer of mercy and receive the gift of salvation through Jesus Christ. At times, he gave in to the temptation of sin, but Joe tried to follow Christ faithfully. Joe said yes to God's offer of love and redemption. When Joe dies, he immediately faces God's judgment. This is called the "particular judgment" because it's given to each individual.

Through his particular judgment upon his death, Joe will either:

1. be granted immediate entrance into heaven;
2. be purified in purgatory before entering heaven;
3. be condemned to hell.

What if Joe Hadn't Heard the Gospel or Been Baptized?

God desires the salvation of everyone and provides for the salvation of the whole world through Christ's death and resurrection (the paschal mystery). When those who are ignorant of Christ respond to God's will, they're responding to Christ. God gives every person the opportunity to say yes to his mercy and salvation.

"The Holy Spirit offers to all the possibility of being made partakers...of the Paschal mystery. Every man who is ignorant of the Gospel of Christ and of his Church, but seeks the truth and does the will of God in accordance with his understanding of it, can be saved." CCC 1260

CCC 668–82, 988–1060

ADULTS

Heaven

Point out that the Church doesn't have a definitive vision of heaven. No one can say how similar or different it will be from the life and world we know or dream of. We only know everyone and everything in it will be perfectly redeemed and in full union with the Trinity (see "The Kingdom of God," below).

Purgatory

Ask the participants if they have struggled with this Church teaching. Emphasize that while no one knows the means or length of this final "suffering," it is a real and possible experience. If necessary, share the following Scripture passages which support it:

- 2 Maccabees 12:43–46

Judas and his soldiers "made atonement for the dead"; this is only logical if purification after death is possible

- Matthew 12:31–32

Some sins are forgiven "in the age to come"

- 1 Corinthians 3:10–17

Salvation from imperfect faith and works is possible, but "only as through fire"

- 1 Peter 1:6–7

Genuine faith is "tested by fire"

Assure them that purgatory is *not* a punishment but a means of accomplishing perfection and justice. Encourage them to consider purgatory as a merciful provision from a loving God who wants salvation for all who truly seek forgiveness and mercy.

Jesus revealed God's great love for us. It's how well Joe loved that will determine what happens at the end of his life. Did Joe repent, accept the love of God, and respond by loving God and others? Or did he refuse to do so?

Heaven, Hell, or Purgatory?

> *"Perfect love will make possible entrance into heaven, imperfect love will require purification, and a total lack of love will mean eternal separation from God."*
>
> United States Catholic Catechism for Adults, p. 153

Heaven
If Joe dies "in God's grace and friendship…perfectly purified," his soul will go straight to heaven (*CCC* 1023). **Heaven** is a place of joy in communion with the Trinity, Mary, the angels, and all the blessed; "the ultimate end and fulfillment of the deepest human longings, the state of supreme, definitive happiness" (*CCC* 1024).

Scripture uses many images to describe heaven—a heavenly city (Revelation 21:10), an eternal dwelling (2 Corinthians 5:1), a glorious wedding banquet (Matthew 22:1–14)—pointing toward supreme happiness that's beyond human understanding.

- *What do you imagine heaven will be like?*

Hell
If Joe has rejected God's love and mercy, he will end up in **hell**, which is "eternal separation from God" (*CCC* 1035). This is possible because God loves everyone, but he gives us **free will**, the freedom to receive or reject his love. Each individual has the choice of their ultimate destiny. Finally and definitively choosing to reject God leads to eternal separation from God in hell.

> *"God predestines no one to go to hell; for this, a willing turning away from God (a mortal sin) is necessary, and persistence in it until the end."*
>
> *CCC* 1037

Purgatory
If Joe responds to God's mercy but isn't free from all attachments to sin, he can be "assured of…eternal salvation" but must go through "purification" after death to "achieve the holiness necessary to enter the joy of heaven" (*CCC* 1030). This final purification is **purgatory**, which involves a "purifying fire" but is "entirely different from the punishment of the damned" (*CCC* 1031). How long this takes likely depends on how much purification Joe needs to be ready to meet God face to face in heaven.

Scripture encourages us to pray for the dead (see 2 Maccabees 12:44). The living members of the Church on earth, the saints in heaven, and the souls in purgatory are united as one Mystical Body in Christ, the communion of saints, and help one another through mutual prayer (*CCC* 954–959).

Praying for the Dead

Praying for our loved ones who have died can bring us comfort. Try praying this prayer for someone you love who has died:

Eternal rest grant unto [name] O Lord. And let perpetual light shine upon [him/her]. And may the souls of all the faithful departed, through the mercy of God, rest in peace. Amen.

The Second Coming of Christ

In the Nicene Creed, Catholics confess that Christ "will come again in glory to judge the living and the dead and his kingdom will have no end." Having defeated evil by his death and resurrection and having ascended to heaven, Christ rules in glory as king. His kingdom is already present on earth as a seed; however, the Church on earth and all

Praying for the Dead

Remind participants, if necessary, that the faithful departed are still connected to us through the communion of saints (see lesson Q15).

of creation anticipate the perfection of Christ's kingdom upon his return, when sin and death will be no more.

With a partner or as a group, look up ways that Jesus describes God's kingdom in the Gospel of Matthew. Share what you find.

The kingdom of God is like...

Matthew 13:24–30	Matthew 13:31–32
Matthew 13:33	Matthew 13:44
Matthew 13:45–46	Matthew 13:47–50

- *Based on these parables, what do you think the kingdom of God will be like?*

What Is the Rapture?
Some Christians expect the **Second Coming** to occur in two phases:

1. a rapture (or catching up) of all Christians to heaven, followed by
2. a time of tribulation on earth until Christ finally comes again.

This is not the teaching of the Catholic Church. Scripture teaches that the living will meet the Lord "in the clouds" as he descends to earth. This catching up of the faithful and Christ's Second Coming are not two distinct events but one (see 1 Thessalonians 4:16–17). Some Christians also expect an earthly thousand-year reign of Christ after his Second Coming. This is based on a literal interpretation of Revelation 20, which the Catholic Church rejects.

The Resurrection of the Body

In the Nicene Creed, we profess that we "look forward to the resurrection of the dead and the life of the world to come." When Christ comes again, he will raise the dead. Joe's soul will be reunited to his body, which will be miraculously transformed by God's infinite power.

Christians believe that the power of death over humanity has been conquered by Jesus' resurrection. Consequently, the human person (body and soul) will be restored for eternal life. We will live forever with God in some beautiful form that will never age, decay, or suffer. Christ's transfiguration and post-resurrection appearances, as well as his presence in the Eucharist, give us a glimpse of this. Mary's assumption, body and soul, into heaven upon her death serves as a promise of our future.

> *"Jesus took Peter, James, and John his brother, and led them up a high mountain by themselves. And he was transfigured before them; his face shone like the sun and his clothes became white as light."*
>
> *Matthew 17:1–2*

- *How do you envision your resurrected body? How does this change how you feel about your current body?*

The Final Judgment

After the resurrection of the dead, "In the presence of Christ...the truth of man's relationship with God will be laid bare" (*CCC* 1039). Joe's particular judgment determines his eternal destiny and won't change. In the Final Judgment, all our actions and their consequences will be known, and their ultimate meaning within the context of God's saving work throughout the ages will be revealed to all. Christ will pronounce judgment on every evil act and reward every good deed with the honor it deserves (see John 5:21–29).

The Resurrection of the Body

Ask if any participants have viewed heaven as only a spiritual, rather than physical, realm. Clarify that this teaching is founded in the revelation that humanity, like Christ, is both soul and body, and that *all* creation is good (Genesis 1).

Invite participants and sponsors to respond to the lesson's questions, "How do you envision your resurrected body? How does this change how you feel about your current body?"

The Final Judgment

Make sure participants can distinguish between their particular judgment and the Final Judgment. Review the lesson's earlier sections if necessary.

The Second Coming of Christ

Share these responses from Matthew, Chapter 13.

The Kingdom of God is (like)...

- Matthew 13:24–30

("good [wheat] seed" sown among weeds) present and fruitful but opposed by the enemy

- Matthew 13:31–32

("a mustard seed") seemingly insignificant or imperceptible yet worthwhile and powerful; see also Mark 4:30–32 and Luke 13:18–19

- Matthew 13:33

("yeast") see also Luke 13:20–21

- Matthew 13:44

("treasure buried in a field") hidden from some and safeguarded by those aware of its existence

- Matthew 13:45–46

("a pearl of great price") priceless, of infinite value

- Matthew 13:47–50

("a net thrown into the sea") offered to all unconditionally, but not universally received

---

The Kingdom of God

Encourage participants to express their vision of God's kingdom as it best suits them. Descriptive prose, figurative poetry, visual artwork, and even musical composition can be effective.

The Kingdom of God

If Joe chose God with his life, he'll enjoy eternal life in the kingdom of God. Humanity, the entire universe, and all creation will be redeemed—transformed in some marvelous manner to share in eternal life.

Waiting for this end shouldn't remove our motivation to improve this present world. On the contrary, faith and hope motivates us to serve others and work for the world's renewal here and now as a sign and beginning of its perfection through Christ (*CCC* 1049, 2820).

What are three things you can do now to prepare yourself for your particular judgment and the Final Judgment?

***Journey of Faith for Adults: Inquiry, Q16* (826252)**
Imprimi Potest: Stephen T. Rehrauer, CSsR, Provincial, Denver Province, the Redemptorists
Imprimatur: "In accordance with CIC 827, permission to publish has been granted on March 7, 2016, by the Most Reverend Edward M. Rice, Auxiliary Bishop, Archdiocese of St. Louis. Permission to publish is an indication that nothing contrary to Church teaching is contained in this work. It does not imply any endorsement of the opinions expressed in the publication, nor is any liability assumed by this permission."

Contributing writer: John L. Gresham, PhD. Editors of 2016 edition: Denise Bossert, Julia DiSalvo, and Joan McKamey. Design: Lorena Mitre Jimenez. Images: Shutterstock and Catholic News Service.

Compliant with *The Roman Missal, Third Edition*.
Printed in the United States of America. 20 19 18 17 16 / 5 4 3 2 1. Third Edition

Liguori PUBLICATIONS
A Redemptorist Ministry

Journaling

Read the question aloud and have participants list their responses in their journal.

Closing Prayer

Close with a recitation of the Lord's Prayer, with particular focus on the words "thy kingdom come."

Looking Ahead

This lesson concludes the inquiry portion of the *Journey of Faith* program. Those who have chosen to formally enter the catechumenate should receive preparation for and instruction on the rite of acceptance or welcoming. Congratulate them on arriving at this milestone. In some ways, this transition is like moving from the dating phase of a relationship to a more serious and exclusive state such as engagement.

Encourage the other participants to continue attending as inquirers and spending time with God in prayer and Scripture. Along with the sponsors, offer to review these materials and to answer any lingering questions or concerns.

Journey of Faith for Adults Inquiry Glossary (alphabetical)

abbey (Q11): The residence of a community of monks or nuns, ruled by an abbot (men) or abbess (women). (See **monastery**.)

acolyte (Q12): An instituted minister who assists the clergy at the altar, primarily by preparing the sacred vessels and distributing holy Communion. Often used interchangeably with *altar server*, a true Catholic acolyte today must be a young man (over 21) and able to proclaim God's word. Hence, most acolytes are in training for holy orders (seminarians).

Advent (Q10): The liturgical season that begins the Church year. It lasts from the fourth Sunday before Christmas to the first evening prayer of Christmas on Christmas Eve. This season anticipates and prepares Christians for the *advent* (literally "arrival" or "coming") of Jesus. Related themes include light, joy, hope, repentance, and expectation. The first part of Advent highlights his Second Coming at the end of time; the final octave (December 17–24), his coming into human history by his birth.

alb (Q11): Latin for "white"; the long, white garment worn by the clergy in liturgies and rites. It is symbolic of the purity received in baptism and required to approach God. In the Mass, acolytes, altar servers, and possibly lectors and other lay ministers may wear albs.

alleluia (Q9): Hebrew for "Praise ye the Lord"; a word used in Christian prayer and recited or sung before the Gospel reading at Mass (except during Lent) to emphasize Christ's presence in the word of God.

altar (Q11): The central table in the sanctuary on which the eucharistic sacrifice is offered. It "represents the two aspects of the same mystery: the altar of the sacrifice and the table of the Lord" (*CCC* 1383).

altar server (Q12): A person who assists the clergy at the altar. Duties may include carrying the cross, candles, or censer; holding the book for the celebrant; and presenting the bread, wine, and water during the offertory. Altar servers can be male or female but must have received their first Communion and be trained. (See **acolyte**.)

ambo (Q11): An elevated pulpit from which the Scriptures are proclaimed during Mass. (See **lectern**.)

Amen (Q8): From the Hebrew, an "expression of agreement or consent, …a solemn expression of belief or affirmation" (*New Oxford American Dictionary*). In Christian tradition, it concludes most prayers as a way to say, "Yes; I believe" to the words and sentiments just expressed. In the Catholic liturgy, the *Amen* after the consecration professes our assent to the actions and mysteries of the Mass, and our *Amen* after receiving holy Communion professes our belief in the Real Presence.

Angelus (Q8): A devotional prayer involving the Hail Mary that recounts the events leading up to Christ's birth and our redemption. It is traditionally recited at 6 AM, noon, and 6 PM (except during the Easter season) and is accompanied by the ringing of a bell.

Annunciation (Q10): The angel Gabriel's announcement to Mary that she was chosen by God and asked to become the Mother of God (Luke 1:26–38). Also, the solemnity celebrating this event, which falls on March 25 in the USCCB's liturgical calendar.

apostolic tradition (Q6): Broadly, the religious, moral, and social teachings of Christ and the Church as transmitted through the apostles. This divine revelation was achieved primarily through oral preaching, writing, passing down authority by episcopal succession, and observing those traditions witnessed and experienced while living with Christ. It includes both Scripture and sacred Tradition. (See **divine revelation** and **(sacred) Tradition**.)

apparition (Q14): A supernatural vision; an "experience in which a person or object not accessible to normal human powers is seen and ordinarily also heard" (*Modern Catholic Dictionary*). To confirm its divine origin, the Church seeks evidence and testimony from those involved before requiring belief or veneration from the masses. There are several well-known apparitions of Christ and the Blessed Virgin Mary.

archbishop (Q11): The chief pastor and head of an archdiocese. (See **bishop** and **diocese.**)

archdiocese: (See **diocese**.)

Ascension (of the Lord) (Q10): Jesus being lifted or "taken up into heaven" after the resurrection (Mark 16:19–20; Luke 24:50–52; Acts 1:9–11). Also, a major feast of the Church year marking this biblical event. In the United States, it is a holy day of obligation and occurs either on the sixth Thursday after Easter (fortieth day) or the following Sunday (seventh Sunday of Easter).

associate pastor (Q12): A priest who assists the pastor of a parish. He "can be assigned either to assist in exercising the entire pastoral ministry for the whole parish, a determined part of the parish, or a certain group of the Christian faithful of the parish, or even to assist in fulfilling a specific ministry in different parishes together" (*Canon* 545.2). Also known as a *parochial vicar*.

Assumption (of Mary) (Q10): The liturgical feast celebrating Mary's entrance, body and soul, into heaven. In the United States, it occurs on August 15 and is a holy day of obligation. It is one of the principal Marian feasts and was proclaimed as a dogma by Pope Pius XII on November 1, 1950.

auxiliary bishop (Q12): An assistant bishop to the main bishop in large dioceses and archdioceses.

baptismal font (Q11): A large basin or small pool which contains the blessed water used for the sacrament of baptism. Each parish church should have a baptismal font set in a prominent and visible place, such as the entrance to the nave or a separate *baptistry*.

basilica (Q11): A church designated as a place of special historical or architectural (artistic) importance. Also, certain ancient churches in Rome and elsewhere, either major or minor, that hold special honor. (See **cathedral**.)

Benediction of the Blessed Sacrament (Q8): A liturgical ritual in which a priest or deacon blesses the people by making the sign of the cross with a consecrated host contained in a monstrance, usually after a period of exposition and adoration. "Benediction is often employed as a conclusion to other services, e.g. Vespers, Compline, the Stations of the Cross, etc., but it is also still more generally treated as a rite complete in itself" (*The Catholic Encyclopedia*). (See **Eucharistic Adoration**.)

Bible (Q5): A collection of books—seventy-three in the Catholic canon—accepted as the inspired, authentic account of God's self-revelation and plan of salvation for the human race. It is divided into the Old Testament and New Testament. Also known as sacred Scripture or the (Christian) Scriptures. (See **testament**.)

bishop (Q11): The chief pastor and head of a specific diocese. According to the Second Vatican Council, the bishop is called to "eminently and visibly take the place of Christ himself, teacher, shepherd and priest, and act in his person" (Dogmatic Constitution on the Church *[Lumen Gentium]*, 21). In communion with the pope, the bishops are the successors of the apostles as leaders of the Church and custodians of divine revelation.

brother (religious) (Q12): A man who is a member of a religious institute but is not ordained. The *Catechism* states that religious life is "one way of experiencing a 'more intimate' consecration, rooted in Baptism and dedicated totally to God" (*CCC* 916).

canon (Q5): The authentic and established collection. The canon of Scripture (biblical books) was declared at the Council of Trent (1545–63).

canonization (Q15): The final, infallible declaration by the pope that a person is a saint, in heaven, and worthy of veneration by all the faithful. This step is normally preceded by beatification and the authentication of a miracle ascribed to his or her intercession.

cantor (Q12): The music minister, perhaps a member of the choir, who leads the congregation in song at Mass and other liturgies. He or she proclaims the *responsorial psalm*, any chants or antiphons not sung by the clergy, and announces the hymns.

cardinal (Q12): According to canon law, those who "constitute a special college which provides for the election of the Roman Pontiff...The cardinals assist the Roman Pontiff either collegially...or individually when they help the Roman Pontiff through the various offices they perform" (Canon 349). The title of *cardinal* is honorary, and cardinals are normally bishops.

catechism (Q1): A summary of religious teachings for the purpose of instruction; specifically, the work containing the basics of Christian doctrine. The *Catechism of the Catholic Church* (*CCC*) was commissioned by a synod of bishops in 1986 and first published in English in 1994 for the purpose of "faithfully and systematically present[ing] the teaching of Sacred Scripture, the living Tradition of the Church and the authentic Magisterium" (*Fidei Depositum*, III).

catechist (Q1): Someone who instructs and forms others in the Christian faith, often in preparation for a sacrament or through continuing religious education or adult faith formation.

catechumenate (Q1): From the Greek for "being instructed"; the RCIA period during which those who are preparing for initiation and/or full reception are formed in the Catholic Christian faith. Unbaptized participants are called *catechumens*; baptized participants are called *candidates*. During this period, both are trained in the Christian life through doctrinal study and participation in liturgy and prayer. As their faith grows and develops, they achieve a personal, interior conversion.

cathedral (Q11): From the Latin for "chair"; The bishop's official parish or "home" church, from which he presides and his seat of authority resides. "It is the mother church of a diocese and its clergy have precedence" (*Modern Catholic Dictionary*).

chancery (Q11): The official location of the bishop's administrative offices and programs. Possibly known as the *diocesan curia* or *Catholic Center*.

chaplet (Q8): "Beads strung together on which prayers are counted as they are recited," such as a rosary; also, the series of prayers recited on such beads (*Modern Catholic Dictionary*). One such example is the *Chaplet of Divine Mercy*.

chasuble (Q11): The sleeveless, outermost garment worn by priests and bishops in the celebration of

Mass. Its color and decorative symbols correspond with the liturgical feast or season and reflect its themes.

Christmas (Q10): The solemnity of the Nativity of the Lord, a holy day of obligation celebrated on December 25. Also, the liturgical season lasting from the vigil on Christmas Eve to the feast of the Baptism of the Lord. Its liturgical color is white or gold, and its principal themes are light, joy, and life (Incarnation and birth).

Church (Q13): The visible religious society founded by Jesus Christ under St. Peter and his successors. The purpose of the Church is to preserve and proclaim Jesus' teachings and to make present his sacrifice and sacraments for the salvation of all. While *the Church* is commonly used to refer to the institutional Catholic leadership, it is primarily the people of God united "by faith and Baptism" (*CCC* 804).

Church year (Q10): The annual sequence of seasons, liturgies, and feasts in the Church which "unfolds the whole mystery of Christ" (*Sacrosanctum Concilium,* 102). It begins with the first Sunday of Advent followed by the Christmas season, Ordinary Time, Lent, the Triduum, and the Easter season, then ends with the final weeks of Ordinary Time. Also called the *liturgical year.*

cincture (Q11): A belt or cord; often white, ropelike, and ornamented with tassels. Clergy members and ministers wear them around the waist over their alb.

cloister (Q11): From the Latin for "enclosed"; residences of men or women religious which restrict the free entry of outsiders to promote a life of prayer and reflection within the monastic community living there. Also, certain structures within the area, such as a quadrangle, especially those reserved for the members.

communion of saints (Q15): The entire Church united as one Mystical Body in Christ, including the Church on earth, the faithful departed in purgatory, and the saints in heaven. This communion is distinct from the body of canonized saints. (See **Mystical Body of Christ**.)

conclave (Q12): From the Latin for "with key"; the enclosed (private) meeting of the cardinals in Rome while electing a new pope. The conclave was instituted by Gregory X in 1274 to avoid interference from the outside world during this process.

consecrated (men and women) (Q12): Members of the faithful who "are totally dedicated to God" and "strive for the perfection of charity in the service of the kingdom of God...through vows or other sacred bonds" (*Canon* 573). These include (religious) institutes of consecrated life and the order of virgins. (See **religious (man or woman)**.)

consecration (Q9): The moment in the Mass when the bread and wine are changed into the Body and Blood of our Lord. According to the *Catechism,* "The Eucharistic presence of Christ begins at the moment of the consecration and endures as long as the Eucharistic species subsist" (*CCC* 1377).

covenant (Q5): A solemn and sacred agreement between parties that binds each side to perform certain duties and is intended to be eternal and unbreakable. In the Old Covenant, God promised the Israelites (through Abraham) protection, peace, and nations of descendants with their own land, but they continually broke their agreement. The New Covenant, established through Christ, fulfills the Old, offering salvation and the kingdom to all humanity. (See **testament**.)

convent (Q11): The building in which a community of religious sisters live.

creed (Q8): From the Latin for "I believe"; a basic statement and summary of communal belief and an instrument of institutional unity. Specifically, the ritual prayers used to profess one's belief in the Catholic faith. The Church commonly uses two creeds: the *Nicene Creed* and the *Apostles' Creed.*

crucifix (Q11): A cross adorned with the image (body) of Jesus as the suffering Savior. Blessed crucifixes are sacramentals, a revered object of private or public devotion, and a reminder of the redemptive suffering of Christ.

dalmatic (Q11): "An outer liturgical garment worn by a deacon at Mass and in solemn processions. It has wide short sleeves, reaches to the knees, and is open at the sides" (*Modern Catholic Dictionary*). The deacon's dalmatic often matches the celebrant's chasuble (liturgical feast or season) in color and material.

deacon (Q12): A member of the clergy who is ordained to one of the ministerial orders of the Church along with priests (presbyters) and bishops. In imitation of Christ, the deacon is called to be "a servant in a servant-Church" (USCCB, "Frequently Asked Questions About Deacons"). Deacons minister to the corporal and spiritual needs of the community and assist in preaching the word of God. They can administer baptism; witness marriages; and preside at funerals, Benediction, and other services (*CCC* 1569–71 and Dogmatic Constitution on the Church *[Lumen Gentium]*, III.29). (See **transitional deacon** and **permanent deacon**.)

deanery (Q11): A subdivision of a diocese which consists of a group of parishes supervised by an appointed *dean.*

diocese (Q11): "A community of the Christian faithful in communion of faith and sacraments with the bishop ordained in apostolic succession" (*CCC* 833). A diocese serves a specific geographical area, is led by a bishop, and consists mainly of parishes. If the territory is large or significant, it may be distinguished as an *archdiocese* and its shepherd an *archbishop*.

diocesan priest (Q12): A priest who is ordained into the service of a specific diocese/bishop and commits himself to that authority and group of people. His work is often within a parish or administrative setting and pastoral or ministerial in nature.

director/coordinator of religious education (Q12): A member of the faithful, usually a trained catechist or theology graduate, who manages the religious formation of parish members. They often oversee a variety of religious-education, faith-formation, and sacramental-preparation programs for adults and children, such as RCIA, PSR, and children's liturgy. They may also train and support the catechists and coordinate with the clergy and other ministers and staff, such as school principals, youth ministers, and Bible-study leaders. Sometimes called a *pastoral associate*.

Divine Office: (See **Liturgy of the Hours**.)

divine revelation (Q6): God's gradual self-communication to humankind through "His words and deeds, His signs and wonders" (Dogmatic Constitution on Divine Revelation *[Dei Verbum]*, I.4; see *CCC* 50–53). It is separate from and beyond humanity's natural capacity to seek and know God. It includes both sacred Scripture and sacred Tradition.

divinely inspired (Q5): Influenced by the Holy Spirit to convey the truths which God intends. The authors and books of the Bible are considered *divinely inspired* and instruments of divine revelation, having or being written through the grace of the Spirit.

dogma (Q14): An official doctrine (teaching) of the Church that cannot be disputed or denied. The *Catechism* states that "the Church's Magisterium exercises the authority it holds from Christ to the fullest extent when it defines dogmas, that is, when it proposes truths contained in divine Revelation or also when it proposes...truths having a necessary connection with these" (*CCC* 88).

doxology (Q3): A prayer of thanks and praise to God; in Catholic Tradition, the *major (greater) doxology* refers to the *"Gloria"* proclaimed in the Mass, and the *minor doxology* refers to the more common Glory Be prayer recited in the rosary.

Easter (Q10): The primary and greatest Christian feast celebrating the resurrection of Jesus Christ. Its date is movable and closely linked to the Jewish Passover (between March 22 and April 25). Also, the liturgical season lasting fifty days from Easter Sunday to the solemnity of Pentecost. Its color is white or gold, and its principal themes are joy (rejoicing and praise), eternal life, and salvation (redemption and freedom).

Easter candle (Q11): A large, decorated candle symbolic of the risen Savior, the Light of the World. It is blessed on Holy Saturday and lit during the Easter season as well as for the rite of baptism. Also called the *paschal candle*.

epistle (Q5): A letter; specifically, the twenty-one works that make up a large part of the New Testament. The epistles are commonly divided into the Pauline letters and the Catholic letters. The Pauline letters were written by Saint Paul or by his disciples in his name. The Catholic letters were written to a more universal audience by various authors from AD 65 to about 95.

eschatology (Q16): Greek for "last things"; the part of theology focused on the afterlife: death, judgment, heaven, hell, purgatory, the resurrection of the body, and the Second Coming of Christ.

Eucharist (Q9): Greek for "thanksgiving"; the sacrament through which Christ's self-sacrifice is made present and bread and wine become his Body and Blood. It was instituted by Jesus at the Last Supper and is celebrated by the Church today in the Mass. According to the *Catechism*, the "source and summit of the Christian life" (*CCC* 1324). Also, the liturgy through which the sacrament is conferred (i.e. the Mass). Also, the consecrated Body and Blood themselves.

Eucharistic Adoration (Q7): A devotion in which one venerates and prays before the Eucharist, either in the tabernacle or exposed in a monstrance on the altar or in a chapel, such as after Benediction. Commonly a Catholic will spend a "holy hour" in such devotion. (See **Benediction of the Blessed Sacrament**.)

extraordinary minister of holy Communion (Q12): A trained lay man or woman who is delegated to assist the clergy in distributing the Eucharist during Mass and may take Communion to the sick and homebound.

faith (Q2): From the Latin for "belief"; the gift of God to trust and accept the word of another by virtue of his or her authority. *Divine* or *religious faith*—knowing and living like we are loved and cherished by God—is both a grace (supernatural gift) and a human act or response. "'Faith *seeks understanding*'; it is intrinsic to faith that a believer desires to know better the One in whom he has put his faith... The grace of faith opens 'the eyes of your hearts' to a lively understanding of the contents of Revelation..." (*CCC* 158). Faith is also a theological virtue (see *CCC* 1812–16 and **lesson M6**).

The term "the faith" may signify the collective doctrine and traditions of the Church as well as the collective beliefs of its members.

feast (day) (Q10): A day or liturgy designated for remembering and celebrating a saint, divine person, or event of special significance to the Church. The

Catholic Church identifies three classes of feasts—memorial, feast, and solemnity—in ascending order of importance. Some memorials are optional, and some solemnities are holy days of obligation.

Final Judgment (Q16): The final encounter with Christ during which all of humanity will be judged and the just and the unjust are eternally separated. "The Last Judgment will reveal even to its furthest consequences the good each person has done or failed to do" (*CCC* 1039). This general judgment is distinct from a person's particular judgment and is revealed in the New Testament. Also called the *Last Judgment* or *Judgment Day*. (See **Second Coming**.)

free will (Q16): Humanity's authentic capability, uniquely bestowed to us by God, to act "according to a knowing and free choice that is personally motivated and prompted from within, not under blind internal impulse nor by mere external pressure" (Pastoral Constitution on the Church in the Modern World *[Gaudium et Spes]*, I.17). This freedom allows us to cooperate with divine grace and choose the good, but also to commit mortal sin and ultimately reject God. Free will neither suggests self-determination (in the sense of creating one's own truth or salvation) nor denies the possibility of predestination (in the sense of God's foreknowledge; see Romans 8:29–30 and *CCC* 600).

friary (Q11): The residence of a community of religious brothers or *friars*, especially those belonging to one of the mendicant orders (Franciscans, Dominicans, Carmelites, Augustinians, and Servites).

gathering space: (See **narthex.**)

genuflection (Q8): Bending down upon the right knee as an act of reverence; it often includes making the sign of the cross. Catholics *genuflect* before Christ's presence in the Eucharist—whether in the tabernacle or exposed in a monstrance—and upon entering and leaving their pew before and after Mass.

Gloria (Q9): An ancient hymn of praise that begins with the song of the angels from Luke's Gospel account of Christ's birth: *Gloria in excelsis deo*, translated "Glory to God in the highest" (See **doxology.**)

godparent (Q1): Someone who is chosen by the catechumen or parents of the child being baptized to serve as a mentor in the faith. A godparent must be at least sixteen years old, an actively practicing Catholic, and willing to take on the commitment of walking alongside the newly baptized on the road of Christian life. In the RCIA, godparents must be chosen prior to the rite of election (*RCIA* 123).

Gospel (Q5): "Good news," one of the four divinely inspired accounts of the life, teaching, suffering, death, and resurrection of Jesus. In the Bible, the four *Gospels* are the books of Matthew, Mark, Luke, and John. In a broader sense, the collective "teaching or revelation of Christ" (for instance, *gospel* values *[New Oxford American Dictionary]*).

hallowed (Q8): Literally, "made holy." To *hallow* something (such as God's name) is to recognize and treat it as holy, to honor and revere it.

heaven (Q16): Eternal life with God and the saints. Heaven is the goal of all human life, "the ultimate end and fulfillment of the deepest human longings, the state of supreme, definitive happiness" (*CCC* 1024).

hell (Q16): A state of "definitive self-exclusion from communion with God and the blessed...eternal separation from God" (*CCC* 1033, 1035). To be in hell after death requires a person to die in mortal sin and his or her free choice to reject God's merciful love and refuse to repent.

holy (Q15): Set apart for the sake of God's kingdom and worthy of honor and imitation. In reference to people, *holiness* or "sanctity" implies strength in virtue rather than perfection in conduct. This closeness to God especially refers to the saints in heaven. In reference to objects, "holy" implies a blessed status (for instance, sacramentals).

holy day of obligation (Q10): A day set aside for worship and relaxation. This includes each Sunday of the year and other feast days (solemnities) designated by the Church. All Catholics are required to participate in the Mass and avoid unnecessary work or business on these days (*Canons* 1246–48).

Holy See (Q12): The official residence of the pope or the power of the pope as supreme pontiff. Also, the tribunals and congregations that assist him in Church governance. Also known as the *Apostolic See*. (See **Roman Curia.**)

holy water (Q11): Water that is blessed by the clergy for use by Catholics. It is used most often to make the sign of the cross while blessing oneself. Holy water is a reminder of baptism and symbolic of spiritual cleansing.

Holy Week (Q10): The week before Easter beginning with Palm (Passion) Sunday and including the Triduum of Holy Thursday, Good Friday, and the Easter Vigil. (See **Triduum.**)

homily (Q9): A sermon or address that explains the Scripture readings and how to apply them and/or instructs the faithful in Christian doctrine and living. Given as part of a Liturgy of the Word in the Mass or another rite, usually by the presider.

ichthys (Q4): A Greek acronym (*ΙΧΘΥΣ*) that translates to "Jesus Christ, Son of God, Savior." From the Greek word for "fish," the animal's symbol also served as a secret identifier of early Christians.

icon (Q8): A sacred image, usually of our Lord or a saint, that is reverenced and often associated with a particular devotion. Icons are rendered or more properly "written" after a period of penance and prayer. Known as doors or "windows to the divine," icons enhance religious contemplation and are rich in symbolism.

immaculate conception (Q10): The dogma that the Virgin Mary was preserved from sin by a singular grace and privilege at the first instance of her conception. The feast is celebrated as a holy day of obligation on December 8 and was declared by Pope Pius IX in 1854 in *Ineffabilis Deus*.

Incarnation (Q3): The act of God's being "made flesh" through the conception of Jesus within Mary's womb at the Annunciation. It revealed the Son to the world and God's plan of mercy and salvation. It is most strongly celebrated at Christmas.

inerrant (Q5): Without mistakes or error; "incapable of being wrong" (*New Oxford American Dictionary*). For example, the truths revealed in the Bible are *inerrant*.

infallibility (Q12): The doctrine that the Church, through the gift of the Holy Spirit, is preserved from the possibility and liability of error in teaching on matters of faith and morals. "In order to preserve the Church in the purity of the faith handed on by the apostles, Christ who is the Truth willed to confer on her a share in his own infallibility. By a 'supernatural sense of faith' the People of God, under the guidance of the Church's living Magisterium, 'unfailingly adheres to this faith'" (*CCC* 889; see also Dogmatic Constitution of the Church [*Lumen Gentium*], 12). The pope himself enjoys this infallibility by virtue of his office; it is also present in the body of bishops when, in communion with each other and the pope, they exercise the supreme teaching office (magisterium) in defining doctrine (dogma) of faith and morals (*Lumen Gentium*, 25). Examples of infallible teachings are the canonization of saints and the Immaculate Conception of Mary.

inquiry (Q1): The first period of the RCIA process. Its purpose is to introduce *inquirers* to the faith and gospel values and to aid them in discerning their intention to enter the catechumenate. During this time, inquirers will learn about Christ, the Church, and the Christian way of life, as well as build an awareness of God's personal love and presence.

intercession (Q14): Invoking a holy person in prayer for the purpose of attaining his or her mediation, thereby strengthening one's request to God. Private veneration of and intercession to the faithful departed is a common part of Catholic tradition, but *public* (liturgical) acts and prayers are reserved to canonized saints. The efficacy of their intercession is understood to come from their proximity to Christ. (See **canonization**.)

introductory rites (Q9): The rites that begin the Mass. They include the entrance chant, the Sign of the Cross, the greeting from the celebrant, the penitential act, the *"Gloria,"* and the Collect. The Liturgy of the Word follows.

laity (Q12): The members of the Church who are not ordained clergy or consecrated to a religious institute. The laity are called to witness the faith in a special way within the secular world and to evangelize in their families and workplaces. Lay men and women are called to the vocations of marriage and single adulthood.

lectern (Q11): A wood or metal podium from which all nonscriptural readings, songs, and chants are led. In a church, the true lectern is secondary to the main *ambo*.

***lectio divina* (Q7):** Literally "divine reading"; a Catholic devotion in which one prayerfully reads and reflects on a passage from Scripture, usually focusing on a specific word, phrase, or aspect of the scene.

***Lectionary* (Q9):** A book containing the Scripture readings for Mass. Ritual editions are used for proclamation; study versions are used for preparation, study, and prayer. Sundays and some solemnities follow a three-year cycle; weekdays follow a two-year cycle. Readings for the Proper of Saints, ritual Masses, and Masses for particular intentions are also included.

lector (Q12): A trained liturgical minister who proclaims the Scripture readings (except for the Gospel) at Mass and in other sacraments, rites, and liturgies.

Lent (Q10): The penitential liturgical season beginning on Ash Wednesday and ending before the Evening Mass of the Lord's Supper on Holy Thursday. This roughly forty-day period is a time for the whole Church to prepare for Easter by entering the paschal mystery more fully through fasting, prayer, and almsgiving.

litany (Q8): From the Greek for "prayer" and/or "supplication," a prayer consisting of a series or list of petitions, saints, or titles. After each item is recited or invoked, the people reply with a fixed and recurring response, such, "Pray for us." Two familiar litanies are the Litany of the Saints and the Litany of the Blessed Virgin Mary (Litany of Loreto).

liturgical year (Q10): (See **Church year.**) A *liturgical calendar* is published or distributed for a given set of dates, often the current calendar year, by the bishops or other Church authority.

liturgy (Q9): From the Greek; a "public work" or worship of the Church, as distinct from private devotion. It usually refers to the celebration of the Eucharist (Mass) but also includes the other sacraments, Liturgy of the Hours, and other ritual services.

Liturgy of the Eucharist (Q9): The second main part of the Latin rite (Roman Catholic Mass). It begins with the preparation of the gifts and offertory (presentation of bread and wine) and includes the eucharistic prayer, Communion rite, and the hymns and responses therein. It concludes with the Prayer after Communion and is followed by the concluding rites (blessing and dismissal).

Liturgy of the Hours (Q8): A repeating cycle of prayers, psalms, hymns, and readings which mark the various "hours" of the day. Also, the daily, public prayer (liturgy) of the Church apart from the Mass. Also known as the *Divine Office*.

Liturgy of the Word (Q9): The first main part of the Latin rite (Roman Catholic Mass). It includes the proclamation of the word of God, a homily on the Scriptures, the recitation of the Creed, and the offering of petitions (Universal Prayer).

magisterium (Q6): Latin for "teaching authority"; the authority vested in the pope and the bishops in communion with him. This teaching authority is sometimes infallible but always expresses authentic Catholic teaching. For this reason, all Catholics are called to be faithful and loyal to these teachings.

martyr (Q15): From the Greek for "witness"; a person who perseveres in suffering and persecution, typically to the point of death, in dedication to and defense of his or her faith. If true martyrdom is established by the Church, the requirement of a miracle for beatification can be waived. (See **canonization**.)

Mass (Q9): The public prayer and worship of the Catholic Church; specifically, the ritual liturgy which constitutes the sacrament of the Eucharist. In the Mass, the faithful gather to give thanks and praise to God, listen to God's word in sacred Scripture, and are nourished by Christ's Body and Blood in holy Communion.

Messiah (Q4): From the Hebrew for "anointed"; a word meaning "Savior" or "Deliverer," used as a title of Jesus, the Son of God. The Jewish prophets foretold the coming of someone who would overthrow the oppressors of God's people and establish a mighty nation, fulfilling God's covenant with Abraham. Jesus fulfilled all the Messianic prophecies, but not in the political sense expected by many of his time.

miracle (Q4): An event that cannot be explained by natural or scientific laws and is therefore considered the work of a divine agent.

monastery (Q11): A place where members of a religious institute live in seclusion from the outside world. It can apply to communities of men or women, but commonly refers to the home of monks or other religious men who live a cloistered (contemplative) life. (See **cloister**.)

monk (Q12): A male religious who is a member of a monastic community. Common monastic orders in the Church include the Benedictines, the Cistercians, and the Carthusians.

monsignor (Q12): An honorary title given to a priest in recognition of his contributions to the life of the Church.

monstrance (Q8): A sacred vessel constructed of precious metals in such a way that the consecrated host is clearly visible. It is used when the host is exposed for eucharistic adoration and in eucharistic processions. (See **Benediction of the Blessed Sacrament**.)

music minister (Q12): A person, often a trained parishioner, who helps to lead music during the liturgy and other services. Many parishes have a paid music or liturgy director who prepares each celebration; directs the choir, cantors, and instrumentalists; and coordinates with parish staff and key parishioners.

mystagogy (Q1): The fourth and final period of the RCIA process; a period of postbaptismal catechesis that generally lasts from Easter until Pentecost. Its purpose is to allow the newly baptized to reflect on their baptism, learn more about their new faith, and explore the ways they may be called to serve the Church and their parish.

mystery (Q3): A deep truth or reality revealed by God but which remains beyond our full understanding or experience. Mysteries reflect God's infinite nature. Through faith, prayer, and study, we can begin to perceive them. A *mystery* of the rosary is an event in the life of Jesus or Mary on which we reflect for a decade of prayer (one Our Father, ten Hail Marys, one Glory Be).

Mystical Body of Christ (Q13): Collectively, the human members of the Catholic Church, a spiritual body with Christ as its head, as united in the sacraments. The Church is "mystical" because the Church is a mystery (spiritual reality) revealed by God which must be accepted on faith. The Church is a "body" because it is made up of various parts and together form the body of Christ present on earth.

narthex (Q11): "A place of welcome—a threshold space between the congregation's space and the outside environment. In the early days of the Church, it was a 'waiting area' for catechumens and penitents. Today it serves as gathering space…[where] people come together to move in procession and to prepare for the celebration of the liturgy" (USCCB, *Built of Living Stones*, 95). It also functions as a place for fellowship, parish communications, and starting certain rites. Also known as the *gathering space* and, informally, the *vestibule*.

Nativity (Q10): From the Latin for "born"; specifically, the solemnity of Christmas, which celebrates the birth of our Lord Jesus Christ on December 25. The Catholic Church also celebrates other nativities throughout the liturgical year. (See **Christmas**.)

nave (Q11): "The space within the church building for the faithful other than the priest celebrant and the ministers" (USCCB, *Built of Living Stones*, 51). It is not a passive or "audience" space but the main body of the church where the congregation actively participates and is brought together for a singular purpose. It mainly consists of seating, usually rows or sections of pews, but also includes the music ministers and various sacramentals.

novena (Q8): From the Latin for "nine"; a devotion consisting of a series of prayers or services that extends for nine consecutive days (weeks or months). The set number was originally based on the apostles' nine days of prayer between the ascension of Jesus and the Spirit's coming at Pentecost.

nun (Q12): While commonly used to describe any female religious, this term actually applies only to those who live the monastic life or in a cloister that restricts contact with the outside world.

offertory (Q9): The moment in the Mass when the unconsecrated bread and wine are brought to the altar and presented as an offering to God. The assembly's gifts—typically monetary donations placed in a basket—are also collected and brought forward. During this time, the congregation often sings the "Offertory Chant" or "hymn during the Preparation of the Gifts."

Ordinary Time (Q10): The liturgical season(s) of the Church year between the end of the Christmas season and the beginning of Lent, and the Monday after Pentecost until the beginning of Advent. Its liturgical color is green and its name is rooted in "ordered time" because the weeks are numbered. The readings reflect on the mystery of Christ's life and help the faithful grow as a Church.

Palm Sunday (Q10): The Sunday before Easter in the Church year. In the liturgy, a Gospel account of Jesus' entry into Jerusalem is proclaimed, and the faithful wave blessed palm branches to recall this scene and joyfully welcome our Savior and king. The Gospel reading, an account of Christ's passion and death, prepares us for the Triduum.

papal nuncio (Q12): An archbishop who acts as the official Vatican delegate to a country. He holds the diplomatic rank of ambassador.

parish (Q11): A geographical region within a diocese that has been assigned its own church and pastor; one's "home church." Also, the faithful residing in that area, the registered members of that church, and the various buildings used by the community. Some parishes are established to serve Catholics of specific rites, languages, or nationalities. (See *Canons* 515–44.)

parish council (Q12): An elected or appointed group of parishioners who advise and assist the pastor in the work of the parish. Its size, structure, and membership vary but may include parish clergy, ministers, staff, and other leaders as well as religious and lay volunteers. Members "are to be selected in such a way that they truly reflect the entire portion of the people..., with consideration given to the different areas of the diocese, social conditions and professions, and the role which they have in the apostolate" (*Canon* 512.2).

parochial vicar: (See **associate pastor**.)

paschal candle: (See **Easter candle**.)

paschal mystery (Q10): "Referring to the passion, death, and resurrection of Jesus Christ, by which he brought about salvation for all humanity" (*A to Z: A Basic Catholic Dictionary*). These redemptive works are celebrated at every Mass and unfold for the Church throughout the Church year.

pastor (Q12): According to canon law, "the proper (shepherd) of the parish entrusted to him, exercising the pastoral care of the community committed to him under the authority of the diocesan bishop in whose ministry of Christ he has been called to share... he carries out the functions of teaching, sanctifying, and governing, also with the cooperation of other presbyters or deacons and with the assistance of lay members of the Christian faithful" (*Canon* 519).

pastoral administrator (Q12): A man or woman who shares some administrative duties of a parish with the pastor. This is an administrative, not liturgical, role. The celebration of Mass and the sacraments still falls to a priest.

pastoral associate (Q12): A member of the faithful, often a certified and employed layperson, who assists the pastor in the work of the parish. He or she may lead nonliturgical services such as wakes, wedding rehearsals, and prayers. He or she oversees the parish's educational and sacramental programs, provides pastoral guidance, and/or performs administrative duties.

penitence (Q10): Sorrow and repentance for one's sins; a desire to seek and obtain forgiveness and make amends. Similar to *contrition*.

penitential act (Q9): The ritual request for God's forgiveness in the Mass "by means of a formula of general confession" (*General Instruction of The Roman Missal*, 51). It consists of a communal recitation of the *Confiteor*, the threefold chant, "Lord, have mercy," or another prayer.

permanent deacon (Q12): A man who is ordained permanently to the diaconate. Permanent deacons must be qualified and either (1) unmarried and twenty-five years of age or older, or (2) married and age thirty-five or older with the consent of his wife. Once ordained, a permanent deacon cannot marry (if unmarried) or remarry (if married). (See **deacon**.)

person (divine) (Q3): A complete and distinct member of the Trinity. The *substance* or essence of God is united in three persons: Father, Son, and Holy Spirit.

petitions (Q9): Prayers to God by the faithful for specific intentions, especially as offered within the liturgy. They usually include requests for the Church, for those who lead and govern, for the poor and suffering, and for various needs of the community and the whole world. (See **Universal Prayer**.)

pilgrimage (Q7): A "journey to a sacred place undertaken as an act of religious devotion" (*Modern Catholic Dictionary*). The journey is always prayerful and more spiritual than physical—with God rather than the location as the ultimate goal and destination. God's people are a *pilgrim* people—traveling the path toward holiness in and through their lives.

pope (Q12): The bishop of Rome and visible head of the Roman Catholic Church. As the successor of St. Peter, he serves as the spiritual and administrative leader of the Church. With the bishops in communion with him, he shepherds all the faithful, and by extension, the whole world.

prayer (Q7): "The raising of one's heart and mind to God" (St. John Damascene; *CCC* 2559). There are many ways to pray, and we are called to participate in both private prayer and prayer as part of our Church community. Prayer involves communicating with God, whether through recitation, informal conversation, meditation, act or gesture, or active listening. Types of prayer include blessing and adoration, petition, intercession, thanksgiving, praise, and contrition.

priest (Q12): A member of the clergy who is called to serve the faithful in communion with, and under the leadership of, a bishop. "The office of priests…shares the authority by which Christ builds up, sanctifies and rules his Body. … [Priests] are conformed to Christ the Priest in such a way that they can act in the person of Christ the Head" (Decree on the Ministry and Life of Priests [*Presbyterorum Ordinis*], 2). "By the power of the sacrament of Orders…they are consecrated to preach the Gospel and shepherd the faithful and to celebrate divine worship" (Dogmatic Constitution on the Church [*Lumen Gentium*], 28). They can celebrate the Mass, hear confessions, anoint the sick, impart blessings, and, if permitted by the bishop, to confirm, consecrate, and dedicate (Canon 1169). (See **diocesan priest** and **religious priest**.)

(responsorial) psalm (Q9): A sacred hymn or song, usually from the Book of Psalms in the Old Testament. At Mass, the *responsorial psalm* is sung or chanted after the first reading in a call-and-response format: The verses are proclaimed by the cantor or lector, and the refrain is repeated by the congregation.

purgatory (Q16): The state of eternal life in which those who have been judged worthy of heaven but are imperfect at the time of death undergo a final purification. "The sufferings in purgatory are not the same for all, but proportioned to each person's degree of sinfulness. Moreover, these sufferings can be lessened in duration and intensity through the prayers and good works of the faithful on earth" (*Modern Catholic Dictionary*).

purification and enlightenment (Q1): The third period of the RCIA process which immediately precedes initiation or reception into the full communion. It nearly always coincides with the Lenten season and is a time of "intense spiritual preparation, consisting more in interior reflection than in catechetical instruction" (*RCIA* 139).

RCIA (Q1): The *Rite of Christian Initiation of Adults*; the process of becoming a member of the Catholic Church for unbaptized individuals above the age of reason. Each of the four periods—inquiry, catechumenate, enlightenment, and mystagogy—has its own purpose and proper rites. However, the journey officially begins with a participant's entry into the catechumenate and culminates in the celebration of the sacraments of initiation.

Real Presence (Q9): The Catholic dogma, declared at the Council of Trent, that the Eucharist objectively and fully contains the Body, Blood, soul, and divinity of Christ. This presence is not symbolic but actual, substantial, immediately effectual, and everlasting.

reconciliation chapel (Q11): A private room or space reserved for the sacrament of penance. It should include a chair for the minister, a kneeler and chair for the penitent, and a screen or fixed grille for anonymity. The penitent has the option, but is not required, to confess face to face. This area should be in a "visible and accessible" place in the church (*Built of Living Stones*, USCCB, 103). Also called a *confessional* or *reconciliation room*.

rectory (Q11): The residence of the priests serving a parish.

religious (man or woman) (Q12): A member of a religious institute that has taken vows (usually of poverty, chastity, and obedience) in order to follow Christ more faithfully. "As a consecration of the whole person, religious life manifests in the Church a wonderful marriage brought about by God, a sign of the future age. Thus the religious brings to perfection a total self-giving as a sacrifice offered to God" (*Canon* 607). (See **brother** and **sister**.)

religious priest (Q12): Unlike a diocesan priest, a priest who belongs to a religious institute and usually lives with his community rather than in the parish. Religious priests take the same vows as others in their order or congregation, including poverty, chastity, and obedience.

rite (Q1): A religious ceremony, usually marked by fixed prayers and actions, that signify a divine work or change in the recipient. Also, the manner and form in which the ritual is performed.

Roman Curia (Q12): The officials and offices who assist the pope in the day-to-day handling of Church matters and resources. (See **Holy See**.)

***Roman Missal, The* (Q11):** The book of prayers and directives for the celebration of the Mass and other liturgies. Formerly called the *Sacramentary*.

rosary (Q8): A devotion consisting of a series of prayers and meditation on events (called *mysteries*) in the life of Jesus and Mary. Also, the loop of beads on which the prayers are counted. There are four sets of mysteries: the Joyful, Luminous, Sorrowful, and Glorious.

sacramental (Q8): Visible or tangible signs that draw us to God and aid us in worship and devotion. A common part of Catholic prayer and practice, they may consist of sacred actions, blessings, or blessed objects. Familiar sacramentals are candles, ashes and palms, Bibles, crucifixes, medals, statues, and religious art. Their efficacy depends on "the person who uses them and of the Church in approving their practice" (*Modern Catholic Dictionary*).

sacraments of initiation (Q1): The sacraments received to become a full member of the Catholic Church: baptism, confirmation, and the Eucharist.

(sacred) Tradition (Q6): All the divine revelation not included in sacred Scripture but passed on from one generation of believers to the next. Tradition is authoritatively maintained and continued through the Church by the magisterium.

sacristy (Q11): A room in or near the church where the ministers prepare for liturgical services, put on their vestments, and store sacred vessels and other materials.

saint (Q14): A person who has lived a holy life of heroic virtue, is in heaven, and is honored by the universal Church. Broadly, all the faithful disciples of Christ. (See **canonization**.)

salvation history (Q5): God's saving plan and works as recounted through time, people, and events. It especially involves humanity's relationship with God and the history of our faith, including the two covenants and events in Scripture.

sanctuary (Q11): The raised area in the front or center of the church where the altar, ambo, celebrant's chair, and often the tabernacle are located. The main focus and actions of the Mass occur in this area, and it is often reserved for the ministers.

sanctuary lamp (Q11): A light or candle, often red, kept burning at all times whenever the Blessed Sacrament is present. This light can usually be found near the tabernacle.

(sacred) Scripture (Q5): From the Latin for "writings"; a religious work considered to be sacred or holy, such as the Hebrew Scriptures. Specifically, the books of the (Catholic) Christian Bible. (See **Bible.**)

Second Coming (Q16): The return of Christ and fulfillment of God's kingdom in the "new heavens and a new earth" (Isaiah 65:17, 2 Peter 3:13, Revelation 21:1). Scripture reveals that some worldly tribulation will precede this event. Also called the *end times*. (See **Final Judgment**.)

shrine (Q11): A sacred place, typically the physical or geographical location of a holy object or event such as a statue, image, relic, miracle, apparition of the Blessed Virgin Mary, or where a saint was born, buried, or lived.

sister (religious) (Q12): A woman who is a member of a religious order. The *Catechism* states that religious life is "one way of experiencing a 'more intimate' consecration, rooted in Baptism and dedicated totally to God" (*CCC* 916).

sponsor (Q1): A member of the parish who guides and encourages a catechumen or candidate throughout the RCIA process. The sponsor affirms the participant's readiness and presents him or her to the minister and community in various rites. The requirements for an RCIA sponsor are the same as for a baptismal godparent.

Stations of the Cross (Q11): A devotion in honor of the passion and death of Christ. It consists of meditating on a sequence of fourteen events from Jesus' condemnation to the laying in the tomb. Most Catholic churches have pictorial stations or crosses attached to the walls around the church depicting each scene. Also called the *Way of the Cross*.

stole (Q11): A long band of material worn around the neck and shoulders, symbolic of the "yoke of the Lord." Priests wear a stole during the celebration of the sacraments. Deacons may also wear a stole, but only diagonally over the left shoulder like a sash.

tabernacle (Q11): A sacred vessel in which consecrated hosts are stored for Adoration and future distribution and consumption. It is often gold or ornately decorated and shaped like a box or tent. The tabernacle should be located in a visible and prominent place in the church, such as the sanctuary.

testament (Q5): A formal agreement or *covenant* used to describe the relationship between God and his Chosen People. The books of the Bible are divided into the Old Testament and New Testament, which correspond to the Old Covenant made with the Israelites through Abraham (Genesis–Malachi) and the New Covenant made with all humanity in Jesus Christ (Matthew–Revelation).

Torah (Q5): The first five books of the Bible, which contain the Jewish Law as revealed to Moses: Genesis, Exodus, Leviticus, Numbers, and Deuteronomy. Also known as the *Pentateuch*.

transitional deacon (Q12): A man who receives the order of deacon as he advances to the priesthood.

Triduum (Q10): Latin for "three days"; the central celebration of the Church year which "marks the end of the Lenten season" (USCCB). While liturgically a single celebration, it includes three evening services: the Mass of the Lord's Supper on Holy Thursday, (Good) Friday of the Passion of the Lord, and the Easter Vigil on Holy Saturday, which commemorates the resurrection.

(Most Holy or Blessed) Trinity (Q3): A collective name for the one, true God; also, the doctrine that states there are three persons in one God, the Father, Son, and Holy Spirit, and that they are eternally united in a communion of love.

Universal Prayer (Q9): The *Prayer of the Faithful* or *General Intercessions* at Mass, when "the people respond...to the Word of God which they have received [and] offer prayers to God for the salvation of all" (*GIRM* 69). The intentions "are announced from the ambo," and this concludes the Liturgy of the Word (*GIRM* 71). (See **petitions**.)

USCCB (Q12): Acronym for the *United States Conference of Catholic Bishops*, the official "group of bishops of [the USA] who jointly exercise certain pastoral functions for the Christian faithful of their territory" (*Canon* 447). It was established after Vatican II as the joint National Conference of Catholic Bishops (NCCB) and United States Catholic Conference (USCC), then merged under its current name in 2001. Within this conference, the bishops "exchange views, consult with one another and cooperate in promoting the common good of the Church" (Pope John Paul II, On the Theological and Juridical Nature of Episcopal Conferences *[Apostolos Suos]*, I.6). (See also Decree Concerning the Pastoral Office of Bishops in the Church *[Christus Dominus]*, III.36–38).

Vatican (Q11): The worldwide administrative headquarters of the Roman Catholic Church and the pope's official residence. This term may refer, collectively, to the buildings, offices, or members within *Vatican City*, the Church's sovereign nation-state located in Rome. (See **Holy See** and **Roman Curia**.)

venerate (Q14): To respect, honor, and revere someone or something holy because of its virtue or blessed status. Catholics venerate Mary and the saints as well as sacramentals such as relics. When the object is God himself, such as in the Eucharist or the cross during the celebration of the Lord's passion on Good Friday, the proper term is worship or *adoration*.

vestments (Q11): Symbolic garments worn by clergy and other ministers during liturgical celebrations.

Way of the Cross: (See **Stations of the Cross**.)

worship (Q14): Due to God alone, an act of adoration and submission to the one who created the world and gives us eternal life. Also, the formal and public rites that effect such acts, specifically the Mass and other liturgies.